Powerful Profits from

CRAPS

Casino Magazine*'s Play Smart and Win*
(Simon & Schuster/Fireside, 1994)

Casino Games Made Easy (Premier, 1999)

*Casino GambleTalk: The Language of Gambling and
New Casino Games* (Kensington, 2003)

Powerful Profits from Blackjack (Kensington, 2002)

Powerful Profits from Slots (Kensington, 2003)

Powerful Profits from Video Poker (Kensington, 2003)

Winning Strategies for Casino Games (Kensington, 2004)

Powerful Profits from Keno (Kensington, 2004)

Ultimate Internet Gambling (Kensington, 2004)

Powerful Profits from

CRAPS

VICTOR H. ROYER

LYLE STUART
Kensington Publications Inc.
www.kensingtonbooks.com

LYLE STUART BOOKS are published by

Kensington Publishing Corp.
850 Third Avenue
New York, NY 10022

First printing: August 2003

10 9 8 7 6 5 4 3 2 1

Printed in the United States of America

Library of Congress Control Number: 2002116572

ISBN 0-8184-0652-6

This book is gratefully dedicated to

Jiřinka Lukášová

"Veni, vidi, vici"—"I came, I saw, I conquered."

—Julius Caesar

Remember this each time you go to a casino.

Contents

Foreword

It is too bad that the game of Craps has lost much of its popularity. There was a time when Craps was the mainstay of American gaming. Virtually every serious gambler knew how to play it, and play it they did!

The game of Craps reached its greatest popularity during the Second World War. Soldiers played it to pass the time at boot camp and between battles. Movies popularized it, such as *Buck Privates* with Abbot and Costello (1941), and later in the 1950s in scenes such as the famous "snake eyes" roll from *Hollywood or Bust* with Jerry Lewis and Dean Martin. In the 1960s, Frank Sinatra and the Rat Pack rolled us in the aisles with laughter in the famed "Copa" room at the Sands in Las Vegas, now legendary, and rolled craps in the casino between shows. Before advances in computer technology permitted the spread of slot machines, video slots and multigame machines, Craps was king. Everyone who would dare to call himself a "gambler" would play Craps. Even today, Craps is considered by many as one of only three casino table games that can be consistently beaten with correct and professional play, a game in which the house edge can virtually be eliminated and certainly minimized.

If you have never played Craps, perhaps you have avoided the game because it looks so intimidating. There are many players standing around, yelling. The game looks like it's played in a big bathtub full of strange markings.

There's a dealer with a long stick and he waves it around like he's trying to hit somebody. Then there is this man in a suit who sits in the middle of the bathtub, with all the chips in front of him. He always looks surly, as if he were some-how lost from the set of *The Godfather*. Two dealers stand on either side of this man, and they put down and pick up chips with such speed that no one can tell who's doing what, how, or when. Have you even wondered what all this means? Did you try to play the game, but were afraid? Or perhaps you didn't play because you just did not want to look silly.

Don't be ashamed. Most people these days know little, or nothing, about the game of Craps. The men who made it so popular at the end of WWII are now mostly gone, and the new casino players are more used to other games—arcade games, video games, computer games, computerized slots, and now video slots. These games are far less intimidating than Craps.

Craps is a social game. Here, you play with people. Lots and lots of people. Other games, such as video slots, arcade games, or computer games, are more solitary. One of the rea-sons why Craps may not be familiar to you is because it has not yet been made into a popular video game. There have been many attempts to do so, but all failed. The one simple reason is that to enjoy Craps, you must play it live—with people, with real dice you can actually hold. None of this is possible on a video game.

In this book, you will find out how to play Craps imme-diately, and easily. There is nothing strange about the game—it only looks that way. You will quickly learn that there are really only three bets to make; this will get you started right away, without any hard learning, or the need to become an expert. Later, as your confidence grows, you may wish to explore other aspects of the game, and get more in-volved.

For those of you who have already played Craps, this book will help you play better, and win more and more often. You will learn to spot the subtle changes that casinos have made to the game, which you may not even notice— unless you learn what to look for, and what it means when you see it.

Finally, you will learn that Craps is one of the best casino games you can find. The house edge against you, if you play correctly, is almost nothing. This alone makes Craps one of the better bets for your gaming dollar.

In these pages, we will demystify the game of Craps. You will learn how to play the game, what pays what, which bets to make and which to avoid and why, and how to maximize your win potential. Finally, you will learn that Craps is, at the core, a very simple game.

Don't be scared to play. Once you play, don't be fooled. Here, in this book, you will find the real answers, and the real truth.

Preface: Why This Book?

This is the third in a series of books I am writing under the general title: *Powerful Profits*. The first was *Powerful Profits from Blackjack,* the second, *Powerful Profits from Slots.* Each of the books in the series begins with this preface: Why this book? It's a question I always ask myself when buying a new book, especially a new book on casino games. I write this preface in each of my books because I wish to answer that question for myself, as well as for you.

When I consider buying a new book on casino games, I always look to see if the book meets these basic four criteria:

1. Does it tell me what is what, what does what, and when, how, and what it pays?
2. Does it explain the game simply so I can understand it immediately?
3. Does it show me a simple strategy so I can play the game wisely, and right away?
4. Does it show me something "new," which other books don't have?

It's a tough task to set for any book. Most books fail on at least one of these items. I always want to know "who, what, why, where, and when," the 5 Ws of the newspaperman's credo. As it applies to gaming books, my item #1, above, is an adaptation of this approach to gaining the most information in the least possible time and space. Many books I have

read do some, but not all of them. Those that are there are
often confusing, because the authors assume that the readers already know something, or know the language of the
casino lifestyle and casino games. I have also written another book, *Casino GambleTalk: The Language of Gambling
and New Casino Games,* in which I provide, for the first
time, a comprehensive glossary of the language, idioms, slang,
and generally used expressions—knowledge of which is required by anyone trying to read, and understand, anything
written about casinos, casino games, or the casino business
or lifestyle. This book was written precisely because I have
found that many gambling books already assume that the
readers know the language of gambling.

What I call item #2 is a little easier to accomplish, and
determine. Most books on casino gambling and games explain the games fairly well. They answer the questions and
supply the mathematics, percentages, frequencies, and all
the other stuff that makes these answers possible. My problem with most books is, however, that these explanations
tend to be too focused on the mathematics and percentages.
In Craps, of course, this is necessary, because the game cannot be explained, or played, without this—but that's not all
that the game is about. Likewise for other casino games. So,
my problem with these books is that often the *explanations*
of the game get bogged down in the desire to *quantify* the
game, while the *purpose* of the explanation may get lost in
the telling. I want to learn the simplest—and quickest—way
to play the game right away.

What I call item #3 is a little easier and a little harder,
both at the same time. Simple strategy, whatever that may
be and however it may apply to the casino game in question, is highly relative to that specific game, or that specific
author's perspective on that game. That's why it is possible
to have more than one book on the same casino game, be-

cause no two perspectives on the same subject are always the same. It's like that story of the glass of water, filled only halfway. Some people see the glass as half full, while others see it as half empty. The first are the optimists among us; the others, the pessimists. This example is a good way to indicate the differences among us, as human beings, as well as the differences among authors and their books. Some authors suggest that casino gambling is a war—you against the casino, or game, or table, or dealer, or whatever. Others assume you want to be a gambler. All of these have a specific place in the arena of casino gambling books, and each contributes to the greater picture of the games we are discussing.

I am, however, often disappointed when I don't find anything that can be called a simple strategy. Sometimes they aren't so simple. In the final analysis, each "simple strategy" becomes the personal perspective of the author; for that reason, if no other, reading more than one book on any game is a good idea. It offers a wider view of the total knowledge available on the game, or subject. Nevertheless, I am still hard-pressed to locate anything I could classify as a universally applicable simple strategy for Craps. There are many strategies offered, but none that fall easily under the category of what I called my item #3. So, in this book, I have devised the simplest, and easiest, and absolutely the best simple strategy. It is as simple as "either-or." With this information at your disposal, you will immediately become empowered to make bets in Craps, and do so wisely, with low house edge and greatest potential for profit, without ever having to learn anything else.

Finally, what I called my item #4, has to do with the differences between books on Craps and their authors' opinions and advice. Is there something "new" in those books? Is there something "new" in *this* book? In many books I have read, there is very little "new" about Craps, and that's understandable. It is a finite and completely defined game. There is very little that can be said to be "new" about it, or the way to play it. This is not necessarily bad. But what is there that *can* be new? Well, the changes to the rules, the way the game is played, the casino payoffs, the game structure, bets offered and not offered, and so on, are all things that can be "new." This book contains information about such changes to the game of Craps, changes that have only recently been implemented. Most books won't have this information, at least not yet. This book explains all the new ways of dealing with the game. I tell you not only *what* they are, but *why* they are, and also *how* this will affect you when you play Craps.

What else is "new"? Well, I have a chapter on what I call The Big Secret. That's my own discovery about Craps, and it's the most powerful reason for this book. Of course, we have a way to go yet before we can get to that. First, we must learn the game the way it should be learned. Without the hype, just the truth, as it actually exists in real casinos—not some theoretical analysis that will mean nothing to your empty wallet. This is the real stuff, the kind of knowledge you must have, from the very beginning, to correct the errors and misconceptions that have plagued the game of Craps in modern times; it will also prepare you for the understanding required to make you a winning Craps player.

So, let's start at the very beginning. Even if you already know Craps, or think you know, perhaps this book will help you sharpen your mind, and your knowledge and skills. If you don't know anything about Craps, or only very little, here is where you will find out all you will ever need to know. We begin with a chapter called "Craps by the Numbers." This is a short listing of everything—the answer to my item #1, above. This is followed by "Introduction to Craps." Here, we will use the information from the first chapter and provide a workable framework for the game of Craps, as it is played in the actual casino. After that, we will dive right in, and find out more about each of the many ways to play Craps.

Good luck, and let's roll dem bones!

Powerful Profits from

CRAPS

Craps by the Numbers

The casino game of Craps is all about numbers. The game revolves around the numbers that can be rolled by two dice. The odds of the game are derived from numbers. Good bets and bad bets are divided by numbers—as are the house percentages for those bets, which determine whether they are good or bad bets. Of course, each "bad" bet for the player is actually a "good" bet as far as the casino is concerned, so it's important that we understand that we are talking from the *player's perspective*. Here, we are discussing Craps as a game from which *we* wish to make profits. Therefore, we won't be concerned about the casinos, even though we will discuss how they make money from the game.

Overreliance on mathematics in gambling is a prescription for disappointment. Just because the theoretical analysis indicates that the mathematics of the game, and its derived odds and percentages, define certain bets as "containing a low house edge," while others are shown as "having a huge house edge," doesn't mean that these bets must be avoided. That is the primary fallacy of most books on casino gam-

bling. Just about every book on Craps that you will find will
state something like this: "To be a winning Craps player,
you must keep your bets only to those that contain the lowest house edge, or no edge, such as free odds." I agree with
the "no edge" part, such as those free odds (which we will
discuss shortly), but why only the "low house edge" bets?
What about all the other bets on the Craps layout? Are they
"bad" bets? Theoretically, based on the mathematics, they
are. A bet where the house edge against you is 9 percent, or
16 percent, is statistically a lousy bet. I wouldn't want to
consistently make bets where I will be guaranteed a loss of
$9 out of every $100, or, worse, a loss of $16 out of every
$100 I bet. But does this mean that these are really "bad"
bets?

The problem we are encountering here is the oldest
problem with all of gambling literature—the general overreliance on mathematical analyses of event-occurrences,
leading to perceptions of percentages for or against. While it
is necessary to have these in order to have a game at all,
your exposure to the game of Craps will be nowhere near as
long as any such empirically derived statistical research
into the mathematics of the game would indicate. Over a
million throws of the two dice, for example, it may be rea-
sonably accurate to state that, under conditions where the
house pays off wagers at less than true odds, a wager on Big
6 or Big 8, for example, will produce a loss of around $9.09
for each $100 wagered. That's about a 9.09 percent house
edge, give or take a few tenths, depending on the statistical
sampling.

Okay, fine. What exactly does this tell us? Well, first it
tells us that anyone wagering on the Big 6 or Big 8 is a sucker.
The reasons for this have only partly to do with this example. A little later, we will find out that these bets can be
made successfully, and far more profitably, *elsewhere* on the

table layout. The real story here is that this statistical sampling—whatever the event may be—is simply inconclusive as far as any Craps player is concerned. When you go to a casino to play Craps, will you play for one million rolls? Most likely, not. Well, then, what good are these statistically derived odds to you? Not much. You may shoot Craps for 10 minutes, maybe 30 minutes, maybe even an hour at a time. During this period, at best, you may see 40–50 rolls—a far cry from one million rolls. Simply put, what all this boils down to is that the statistics in the game of Craps, as indeed in all gambling games, are only good as a *guideline.* These numbers are important to the game, because without them the game could not exist, but they are far less important to you as the player, because you will never play the game long enough for these numbers to have more than a tiny effect on your wins. When you play, you will either win a lot more than the statistical averages of the game indicate, or far less. You will never equate to the expected theoretical average. Therefore, what does it matter if you bet, say, any 7, and face a house edge of over 16 percent? Is it a lousy bet? Yes, it is. Does it *never* hit because it's such a lousy bet? No. If you make this bet, are you an idiot? Statistically, yes. Realistically, no. In the real world, anything is possible. That's why casinos can survive, and that's why players of casino games still have a chance. If everything in the casino always paid off only at those long casino odds, with those heavy casino edges, then casinos would soon die out because people would never come to play. After a while, even the most diehard gamblers would realize that bucking those house odds would lead to financial ruin. The price for that entertainment would just be too high. However, that is not the case. Casinos thrive, and are spreading. Not only because playing casino games is very entertaining, very liberating, and often very profitable, but also because even casual or novice players can, and do, win. Without winners, the theoretical mathematics of the game would simply grind everyone down, and no enjoyment, or winning, would happen.

Consequently, for you to derive the most powerful profits from Craps you need not confine yourself only to the three bets that produce the lowest overall house edge. Instead, you should be aware of what the percentages *are*, what the house edge on each bet *is*, and how this may affect your winnings over a long series of events, but you must not let this control your play. If it does, then Craps will be not only boring, but also not very profitable. Playing Craps in a manner where your bets face only a less than one percent combined house edge may be fine, but if playing this way means you will achieve only an expected value win of around $5 per hour, then that's ho-hum. Highly tedious. A grind. Casinos thrive on grind, *because all their games make money all the time,* in tiny little bits. In Craps, the house edge can be as low as 0.02 percent, which is about two cents of each $100 wagered. Okay, that's good. Wake me when it's over.

The point I wish to make is that playing Craps is supposed to be fun and exciting as well as profitable. This is the way it should be for all the casino games, but especially for Craps. This is a highly social game, where people play with others, and all of us are trying to one-up the casino, the House, that faceless entity that controls the dice game. We all know that the game is structured so that the house will always win—but that doesn't mean that we, as players, can't, or never do, win. Craps can be a very profitable game, and to play it profitably doesn't mean you have to play it in the way most books on Craps advise. You do not have to grind it out on low-edge bets and make wagers that only win little. There are ways of playing Craps that will maximize not only your enjoyment of the game, but also its profitability.

While it is very useful to know which bets are better,

which are the best, and which aren't so good—from the perspective of the game's mathematics—this doesn't mean that such wagers are always off-limits. In fact, some of these wagers are precisely the kinds of bets that will assure you of a nice win. This may seem to fly in the face of all the "traditional" advice for Craps. In some ways, yes it does, but not nearly as much as it may seem. You see, what I preach is not that the mathematics, and statistics, and percentages, are useless, but rather that they are erroneously overvalued when considered in the real world of the very finite, very short slices of event-occurrences of your actual reality. Your exposure to Craps will be short. Nothing like the expected statistical numbers will ever show itself during your time at the game. So what if you make several consecutive bets on-the-hop, and face the theoretical edge of over 16 percent? It can happen, and you can win all of them; even a sequence far longer than is statistically conceivable. Then again, you may lose them all, and an equal sequence of such nonevents can, and will, happen. These are simply the statistical anomalies that happen in everything. Nothing in nature, and certainly not in gambling, ever exactly reflects, or plays to, the theoretical model. And that's why it's possible to win even on negative-expectation games, of which Craps is one. While Craps is one of the better negative-expectation games, it is still, nonetheless, a game where the house will always win, in the long run, all rules and events performing to the theory. Same as Slots. Slots are machines, which have a computer program, and that program will always hold the preprogrammed percentage for the house. Always. All the time. Yet, players can, and do, win on Slots. If they didn't, nobody would ever play them (refer to my book *Powerful Profits from Slots* for more details).

Craps is a game that is statistically unbeatable, yet players often win large amounts of money. I have seen table rolls where the casino lost several million dollars. They lost, and the players won, because trends far from the expected mathematical theory do happen—and happen frequently. This game, in which I was actually playing at the time, cost the casino millions. The players who won the largest portion of this money were *not* the players who were betting the "safe" bets, with the lowest house edge, as most of the traditional books on Craps usually advise. The players who won the most money were those who recognized that a streak was happening—an anomaly in the overall statistics of the game—whereby the "bad" bets were hitting, and making the money. These bets may have been classified as "bad," or "ugly," in the overall accepted literature on Craps, but at that time, this was not true. At that time, *these* were the "good" bets, because that's where the winners were.

This concept is very important for you to remember and try to understand. Very shortly, I will list all the bets on the Craps table, along with their house edge percentages. I will tell you what they are, what they do, how to make them, and what the statistics indicate. In most books on Craps, you will always read that most of these are really ugly bets, and that you should stay away from them. Emotions aside, the real truth is that any of these bets are equally "good" and equally "bad," depending on whether or not they happen to be rolled at the time. As in my example above, that game in which the casino lost millions was only made possible by the following factors:

1. It was a game whose limits were from $25 to $10,000.
2. The shooter held the dice for 55 minutes without seven-out.
3. The dice were rolling numbers and proposition bets with regularity.
4. Only one losing 7 roll occurred, and that was at the 55th minute.

In this game, and many others like it that I have person-
ally witnessed and played in, the way to make powerful
profits did not lie in playing Craps by what the mathematical statistics tell us are the "good" and "bad" bets. In these
games, and indeed in most casino games played every day,
the largest part of the profits lie in being able to throw out
the statistics, dump the math, and go with the roll. Of course,
to do this, you must first not only know what to do, and
how to do it, but also have some skills that allow you to
make the determination of such a monster roll, or at least
know when you are in a mini-roll, and exploit it right then
and there. These may be as short as a few minutes—a roll or
two—or as long as, or longer than, my example. The trick is
in learning how to do this. For that, you will need at least
three items of knowledge:

- First, you need to know what does what, and what it
  pays, and what the house edge is.
- Second, you will need to know all about the game,
  and how it is played.
- Third, you will need to know some kind of a strategy,
  so that you can improve your approach to the game.

Once you have these three, then you can adapt and apply
them to any situation on any Craps table anywhere. You will
learn to avoid the pitfalls, and know when to deviate from the
theory. Therefore, without further comment, here is the "what,"
"how," and "when" of Craps—the game by the numbers.

NOTE ON ODDS

In many books on Craps, and on casino gambling in general,
you will find odds written with a hyphen, such as 3-2, to in-

dicate that these odds are at 3 to 2. This is incorrect. The correct way to write this is to use the colon. Therefore, the correct way to write odds of 3 to 2 is to write it like this: 3:2. This is especially true for Craps, because in this game some casinos will show their odds payoffs as "for 1"—such as, for example, a payoff shown as "30 *for* 1." I will discuss the differences a little later, but the point here is that many authors erroneously write odds "to" in the style that means odds "for." The use of the hyphen in gaming literature always indicates odds "for." The use of the colon always indicates odds "to."

Somehow, in the past ten years or so, either editors have been asking gaming authors to write these in the wrong manner, or perhaps it just happened and no one has commented on the error. This is simply a means of differentiating between gaming statements, and is only meaningful in gaming literature. In my books, and particularly in this book, whenever you see something written as, for example, 30:1, this means that these odds are stated as 30 to 1. Whenever you see odds written as 30-1, this means that these odds are stated at 30 for 1. This will avoid a lot of confusion. However, please do not confuse the standard use of the hyphen when used as a "range" indicator. For example, when we speak of a streak of events from 1 through 30, it would be written as 1-30; or when showing a paired combination, such as 5+5, which could be written as 5-5. This is where your understanding of the *context* of the paragraph or sentence indicates which items mean what, under the specific circumstances of the point being discussed. Wherever possible, I will always try to use the colon as an indicator for odds "to," the hyphen as an indicator of the odds "for," and the plus sign to indicate pairs. I hope this will be clear.

DICE COMBINATIONS

Two dice are used in Craps. Each has six spots. The two dice, together, can roll 36 possible combinations of numbers, as follows:

Number	*Ways it can be rolled*					
7	6, 1;	1, 6;	5, 2;	2, 5;	4, 3;	3, 4
8	6, 2;	2, 6;	5, 3;	3, 5;	4+4	
9	6, 3;	3, 6;	5, 4;	4, 5		
10	6, 4;	4, 6;	5+5			
11	6, 5;	5, 6				
12	6+6					
2	1+1					
3	2, 1;	1, 2				
4	3, 1;	1, 3;	2+2			
5	4, 1;	1, 4;	3, 2;	2, 3		
6	5, 1;	1, 5;	4, 2;	2, 4;	3+3	

For those of you who may not quite understand the mental gymnastics, just remember that if on one roll the die on the *left* hits, say, a 2, and the die on the *right* hits, say, a 3, this is one way one making a 5 total. On the next roll, the die on the left may hit the 3, and the die on the right might hit the 2, and that is still a total of 5. However, here we can clearly see that this particular two-roll sequence hit the number 5 two ways: first as the combination of the two dice as a 2 and a 3, and the second time as 3 and a 2. And so on for the rest of the numbers. Players who may not have a familiarity with the analysis of combined events often have problems figuring this out, but it's actually quite simple. Just think of the two dice as being different, with each one able to combine any of its numbers with the other's numbers, for that particular total. That's all you really need to know. Or just take it for granted that there are 36 ways to make a number out of dice like these.

WHAT AND HOW MUCH

Now, I will list the most common bets found on the Craps table, along with an explanation of what each bet is, how to make it, and its established house edge (rounded off to the nearest whole percentage point, wherever possible). Here's how it will be laid out:

- What:
- Pays:
- True Odds:
- House Edge:
- Means:

The "what" will show what the bet is. The "pays" shows what the bet pays in the majority of casinos. In some places, these pays may be slightly different, but the amounts shown here, in percentages, are virtually standard for most major casinos. I will discuss some of these differences in pays in more detail later on in this book. The "true odds" shows what the actual true event-occurrence really is, and what, therefore, the pays *should be* for Craps to be an even game. Of course, we all know that the casinos must make money from the game, otherwise the game wouldn't exist—but it is still worthwhile to know exactly how badly we, the players, can be exploited in some cases, and on some bets, theoretically speaking. The "house edge" shows the percentage differential between the true odds of the event-occurrence and the pays, thus arriving at the percentage withholding the casinos factor into the game, and these bets, to assure themselves of steady profits. Finally, the "means" explains what the bet means. So, here goes, hold on to your seats—some of these bets really do stink, statistically speaking:

- What: Across the board (Also known as "all across")
- Pays: (depends on the number rolled; see individual numbers, below)
- True Odds: 6:24 (combined)
- House Edge: 3.9 percent
- Means: To wager on all the box numbers—4, 5, 6, 8, 9,

or 10—as a place bet, covering all of these numbers, except the point number. Thus the minimum correct wager is either $27, or $26, all across, depending on whether or not the point number is 6 or 8. If the point number is 6 or 8, your all-across wager would be $26. If the point number is anything else, then your wager would be $27, allowing $6 each for the 6 and 8 for correct payoff. Wins when the numbers are rolled before any 7. Loses when any 7 is rolled. Just to make sure we understand that the All Across bet depends on the point rolled, here is the breakdown: If the point number is 4 or 10, the true odds are 6:21 (6 ways to make a 7 vs. 4 to make a 5, 5 to make a 6, 5 to make an 8, and 4 to make 10 *or* 3 to make a 4, but not both). The house edge here is 3.2 percent. If the point is 5 or 9, the true odds are 6:20 (6 ways to make a 7 vs. 3 to make a 4, 4 to make a 5 *or* 9, 5 to make a 6, 5 to make an 8, 3 to make a 10). The house edge here is 3.7 percent. If the point is 6 or 8, the true odds are 6:19 (6 ways to make a 7 vs. 3 to make a 4, 4 to make a 5, 5 to make a 6 *or* 8, 4 to make a 9, 3 to make a 10). The house edge here is 4.3 percent.

- What: Whirl
- Pays: 16:5
- True Odds: 20:5 (The 7 yields an overall push, there-

fore no-win. If we disregard the 7, the true odds are 24:6, which is the statistical equivalent of 20:5—just in case you are wondering about the details.)
- House Edge: 13.3 percent
- Means: To bet the 2, 3, 11, 12, and the Any 7. It's kind of like the Horn, except here you get Big Red along with it. Also known as "The World." A one-roll wager. To make this bet, which is not marked on the table layout, you toss your money to the stickman and say something like, "Five on the World," or, "Send the five on a whirl." Either way, you will need to bet at least $1 on each of the five bets, so the $5 will most likely be the minimum bet.

- What: Horn
- Pays: 17:4 (depends on number rolled)
- True Odds: 20:4
- House Edge: 12.5 percent
- Means: To bet the numbers 2, 3, 11, and 12, hoping that one of them will be rolled on the next roll. A one-roll wager. Often you can hear people yelling "Horn High-Yo," meaning they are wagering an extra unit on the 11. Also often heard are "Horn-High," meaning the extra chip goes on the 12, or "Horn-High-Low," meaning the extra chip goes on the 2. All are one-roll wagers, with a high house edge over 16 percent on the "high-low" bets.

- What: Hop (also known as "On the Hop")
- Pays: 30:1 (for pairs) 15:1 (for non-pairs)
- True Odds: 35:1 (for pairs) 17:1 (for non-pairs)
- House Edge: 14 percent (for pairs) 11 percent (for non-pairs)
- Means: To make a one-roll wager that the next roll will be a specific combination of the two dice. For example, when a player calls out, "Five-four on the Hop," this means

he is betting that the next roll of the dice will be a total of 9, achieved exactly as called, with one die showing a 5 and the other showing a 4. If this happens exactly that way, the player will win a wager paid as shown above (non-pairs). This wager will lose if any other number total was rolled on that one specific roll, or if the 9 was rolled as a 6, 3 or 3, 6. For pairs, the player must call out a Hop bet for a specific combination, such as: "Little Joe on the Hop," which would be a wager on the total of 4 for that one roll only, achieved specifically, and only, as the pair 2+2.

- What: Any Craps
- Pays: 7:1
- True Odds: 8:1
- House Edge: 11 percent
- Means: To make a wager that the next roll will be any of the three craps numbers: either 2, 3, or 12. A one-roll wager. This bet is mostly used by players on the come-out roll, as a hedge bet. I will discuss hedging bets a little later.

- What: Any 7
- Pays: 4:1
- True Odds: 6:1
- House Edge: 16.67 percent
- Means: To make a wager that the next roll will be the number 7, rolled in any one of the possible six ways. If you wanted to make it a Hop bet, it would then be a one-roll proposition, and you would have to call it out that way, such as, for example: "Five-Deuce on the Hop," meaning a 7 rolled exactly that way.

- What: The Field
- Pays: 1:1 (bonus of 2:1 for the numbers 2 or 12)

- True Odds: 20:18
- House Edge: 5.6 percent
- Means: To make a one-roll wager in the area on the layout marked as "Field." This is a large area, and this is a popular bet. In some casinos, there are bonus pays over and above the 2:1 on the numbers 2 and/or 12. For example, many casinos will pay 3:1 on the number 12, while others may pay 3:1 on the number 2, with the other number remaining at 2:1. If such a bonus is offered in your casino, then the percentages will be affected as follows:

- What: The Field
- Pays: 1:1 (bonus of 3:1 on either 2 or 12, with the other number at 2:1)
- True Odds: 20:19
- House Edge: 2.8 percent
- Means: To wager the one-roll bet on the Field, where the casino pays a bonus of 3:1 on either the 2 or the 12, with the other number remaining at 2:1.

- What: C&E
- Pays: 7:1
- True Odds: 5:1
- House Edge: 12.5 percent
- Means: To make a one-roll wager that either of the numbers 2, 3, 12, or 11 will be rolled on the next roll. It means you are betting on any Craps *and* 11.

- What: Snake Eyes
- Pays: 30:1
- True Odds: 35:1
- House Edge: 14 percent
- Means: To make a one-roll wager on the number 2, as rolled by the two dice in the only possible way of 1+1.

- What: Ace-Deuce (or Acey-Deucy)
- Pays: 15:1
- True Odds: 17:1
- House Edge: 11 percent
- Means: To make a one-roll wager that the next roll will produce the specific combination of a 1 and a 2, for a total of 3. Only possible two ways; see the rolls breakdown shown on page 9.

- What: Yo-'leven (mostly just Yo)
- Pays: 15:1
- True Odds: 17:1
- House Edge: 11 percent
- Means: To make a one-roll wager that the next roll will produce the number 11.

- What: Boxcars
- Pays: 30:1
- True Odds: 35:1
- House Edge: 14 percent
- Means: To make a one-roll wager that the next roll of the two dice will produce the perfect paired combination of 6+6, for the only possible total of 12.

- What: Hard 10
- Pays: 7:1
- True Odds: 8:1
- House Edge: 11 percent
- Means: To make a proposition wager that the number 10, when rolled, will be rolled perfectly, as the pair 5+5. This bet stays in action until it is either rolled that way, 5+5, in which case you win; or it is rolled "easy," meaning one of the other possible combinations that result in a total of 10, in which case you lose; or until you take it "down," or call it "off." More details on this a little later on in this book.

- What: Hard 4
- Pays: 7:1
- True Odds: 8:1
- House Edge: 11 percent
- Means: Means the same as the notes for the Hard 10, except here you are wagering on the combination of 2+2, for a total of 4.

- What: Hard 8
- Pays: 9:1
- True Odds: 10:1
- House Edge: 9.1 percent
- Means: The same as the Hard 4 and Hard 10, except here you are wagering that the number will be rolled as 4+4, for the total of 8.

- What: Hard 6
- Pays: 9:1
- True Odds: 10:1
- House Edge: 9.1 percent
- Means: The same as the other Hardways, except here you want the number to be rolled as a 3+3, for the total of 6.

- What: Big 6 and Big 8 (both pay the same, face the same odds)
- Pays: 1:1 (even money)
- True Odds: 6:5
- House Edge: 9.09 percent
- Means: To make a really stupid bet on the numbers 6 and 8, where all you will get paid is even money—1:1—while the *same bet* made as a place bet on 6 and 8 will earn you a 7:6 payoff, at the much lower house edge.

This, then, covers most of the confusing Craps bets. Now I will list the most popular Craps bets, which are: pass line, don't pass, buy, lay, come, and free odds. The following is a streamlined explanation of what these bets are, and what the house edge is on each of them:

- What: Pass Line
- Pays: 1:1 (even money)
- House Edge: 1.4 percent
- Means: To make a wager on the table layout in an area marked by a double line, defining an area of the betting layout closest to the players and with the word "Pass" written between the lines. This is the pass line, also known as the front line, because it is the first, the front, of the layout as you are standing at the table. Betting in this area signifies that you are betting *with* the shooter, known as the *right-way* bet. On the come roll, you win if the shooter rolls a 7 or 11 and lose if he rolls 2, 3, or 12. If the shooter rolls any of the other numbers—the box numbers, also known as come numbers, or point numbers, you will have to wait to find out whether the shooter will roll that point again before a 7—in which case you win—or he rolls a 7 before the point—in which case you lose. More on this later in this book.

- What: Come Bets
- Pays: 1:1 (even money)
- House Edge: 1.4 percent
- Means: After the point is established, to make a bet in a large area marked as "come" on the table layout. After you make this wager, if the next roll is a 7 or 11, you win. But, if any 7 is rolled, all the right-way bettors lose; so in this case you aren't making this wager because you wish a 7 to show. This bet will lose if a 2, 3, or 12 shows, same as the pass line bets. If any box number is rolled, this will now become your come number. Your wager is now put on that number. Now, your bet wins if that number is rolled again before any 7, and will lose otherwise. You cannot "pick up" or "take down" this wager once it makes it to the come number, just as you

cannot remove your original pass line (or don't pass), bets. However, now that your come bet has made it to your come number, you can take what's called "odds on the come." These are "free odds," and may also be made on the pass line in the same manner. In fact, bets on the pass line and the come both work in the same way. Your come bets are, therefore, like additional pass line bets. They both win, and lose, in the same manner. Both can have free odds wagered on them, up to the maximum of free odds offered by the casino where you are playing.

For example, most casinos will offer what is called "double odds." This simply means that, on both the pass line and come wagers, you can place additional money into action at twice the level of your original bet. Let's say that you wagered $5 on the pass line, and placed a $5 come bet. Then, after the point number was established, you could take $10 in free odds behind your pass line wager, and once your come number was rolled, you could also take $10 odds on your come number. These extra-odds wagers are often called "backing your line bet" or "backing your come," which simply means that you have added extra wagers to your bets. These are traditionally located "behind" your original wager, therefore the moniker "backup" bets.

These free odds wagers are paid by the casinos at the true odds; therefore, there is no house edge on these bets. For this reason, playing Craps where you make the majority of your action on free odds is the best way to play, because on such bets the casino has no edge; you are getting an even game with them. The more free odds the casino offers, the better. For example, some casinos will offer up to 100x odds; this means that you can make a $5 pass line, or come, wager, and back it with up to $500 in free odds, at no house edge. This will, therefore, reduce the overall house edge on this bet to 0.02 percent, meaning that you have lowered the house win expectation to only two cents per each $100 wagered in such a manner. More on this later.

- What: Free Odds
- Pays: true odds, depending on the number and amount wagered
- House Edge: zero percent
- Means: As shown above, you back your bet on pass line and come with extra wagers, up to the maximum offered by the casinos. Some casinos offer double odds, other 3x odds, some 10x odds, and some even 100x odds. By maximizing your action on free odds, you are lowering the overall house edge on those bets and are, therefore, getting a much better game than just about any other casino-banked game. Free odds can be picked up, called off, or taken down, at any time.

- What: Pass Line and Come bets with Single Free Odds
- Pays: depends on the number, and amount wagered
- House Edge: 0.85 percent
- Means: To back your pass line or come bets with the same amount as your initial bet. For example, if you made a $5 wager on the pass line (or come), and then chose to take the free odds, you would add another $5 chip behind your bets. In the case of the come bets, you would toss your odds bet to the dealer and say, "Single odds on the come," in which case the dealer will put your extra $5 chip over your original $5 wager, slightly off-angle, so that the top chip (or chips) somewhat hang over the side of the original chip wager. This indicates that your come bet has $5 in free odds riding. With the pass line, you would place your extra $5 chip behind your original $5 wager, indicating to the dealers that you have taken $5 in free odds backing up your initial $5 line bet. This also shows that you are taking *single*

odds, which is your choice even in casinos which offer 2x, 10x, or even more in available free odds wagers.

- What: Don't Pass and Don't Come
- Pays: depends on the number, and amount wagered
- House Edge: 1.4 percent
- Means: To make a wager that is the *direct opposite* to the pass line and come bets. These wagers win when the pass line and come wagers lose. This is called "wrong way" action (now more commonly known as the "dark side"), and simply means that you will be wagering *against* every other player who has made a bet with the shooter; that is, you are wagering that the shooter will *not* make the point. These bets work exactly the same way as the pass line and come bets—other than the 12, which is a push—except that you put your don't pass wager in the area marked as "don't pass," while when making the don't come bet you simply put your money into the "don't come" betting area. When a number is rolled, the dealer will take your don't come bet and put it behind the number rolled, often topping it with a marker so that it is easily identified as a don't come bet. You win if the 7 is rolled before that number is rolled again. You lose otherwise. Again, this is the exact opposite to the pass line and Come bets.

- What: Don't Pass and Don't Come with Single Odds
- Pays: depends on the number, and amount wagered
- House Edge: 0.82 percent
- Means: To put more money into action as free odds. Same as the examples shown above for free odds, except that here you are betting against the shooter, and exactly the opposite to the pass line and come bets. For the dark side bets, this is called "laying the odds," as opposed to "taking the odds" on the front line (see Chapter Six for more details). All you have to remember is that if you are making

pass line and come bets, all your free odds and your original bets are riding *with* the shooter—meaning that you win if the shooter rolls the point before any 7, and lose otherwise; while when making the don't come and don't pass wagers, you are betting the exact *opposite* to that—you are now betting *against* the shooter, and you will win if the 7 is rolled before the point, or before your don't come number. The free odds bets for the backliner are, however, a little different.

Since after the point is established the "don't" side of the wagers are now a statistical favorite, in order for you to make odds bets, you will now have to wager more, to win less. For example, if the point is 10, and the original wager was $5, and the pass line (or come) bettor is making a single free odds bet of $5, he is betting $5 to win $10. The don't pass (or don't come) bettor would have to make the exact opposite bet, in this example, to wager $10 to win $5. Again, the don't pass and don't come bets, and wagers, work exactly the opposite to the pass line. If the point, or number, are 6 and/or 8, the pass line (or come) bettor bets 6 to win 7 (odds of 6:5 and a payoff of 7:6), while the don't bettor is paid at 5:6, meaning he has to wager $6 to win $5. If the numbers are 5 or 9, the pass line and come pay at 3:2, while the don't side pays at 2:3. If the numbers are 4 or 10, the front line free odds pay at 2:1, while the back-line don't odds pay at 1:2.

Seems confusing? It's not. Here's a hint—think of the pass line and come bets as the "front line," or the top side of a coin. Then, think of the don't pass and don't come bets as the "back line," or the back side of the coin. Now, whenever you consider the front side, remember that you are betting *less* to *win more*. Whenever you are considering the back side, remember that this is the exact opposite to the front side—you must bet *more* to *win less*. This is really a very simple way to put it, but it is accurate. If you think of these

bets exactly this way, you will never become confused. To
calculate your bets, or the value of your odds, simply take the
pass line or come odds, and turn them around. Now, the 6:5
odds for the 6 or 8 becomes 5:6 on the back side. The 3:2 becomes a 2:3, and the 2:1 become 1:2. Just "flip the coin," and
there you are. Simple, right? Well, if it's still a little too much,
then just read on. There will be a lot more discussion on all
of this, and it will make more sense as you read on. Or, if you
are really exasperated, do what I do: stay away from the dark
side, and then you never have to worry about this at all.

- What: Pass Line and Come with Double Odds
- Pays: depends on the number and amount wagered
- House Edge: 0.65 percent
- Means: To make a bet on the pass line, or a come bet
after the point has been established, and then back up the
bet(s) with *double* the amount of the original wager. Same
principle as with single odds, but here you are making a
bet of double free odds, and this therefore further dimin-
ishes the house edge on these bets. This can be done for as
many-times-odds as the casino offers. Below, we will see
some of the most common such wagers, and odds offered,
and their impact on the overall house edge for these bets.
The "don't" side has virtually the same house edge (with
only a few one-hundredths differential, which is statistically insignificant).

- What: Pass Line or Come with Triple Odds
- Pays: depends on the number and amount wagered
- House Edge: 0.46 percent
- Means: To make the pass line or come wagers, and back
this with three times the amount of the original bet as free
odds. The "don't" side has virtually the same house edge
(with only a few one-hundredths differential, which is statistically insignificant).

- What: Pass Line or Come with Five Times Odds
- Pays: depends on the number and amount wagered
- House Edge: 0.32 percent
- Means: To make the pass line or come wagers, and back this with five times the amount of the original bet as free odds. The "don't" side has virtually the same house edge (with only a few one-hundredths differential, which is statistically insignificant).

- What: Pass Line or Come with 10 Times Odds
- Pays: depends on the number and amount wagered
- House Edge: 0.175 percent
- Means: To make the pass line or come wagers, and back this with ten times the amount of the original bet as free odds. The "don't" side has virtually the same house edge (with only a few one-hundredths differential, which is statistically insignificant).

- What: Pass Line or Come with 100 Times Odds
- Pays: depends on the number and amount wagered
- House Edge: 0.02 percent
- Means: To make the pass line or come wagers, and back this with 100 times the amount of the original bet as free odds. The "don't" side has virtually the same house edge (with only a few one-hundredths differential, which is statistically insignificant).

- What: Place Bet on 6 or 8 (that they *will* be rolled before a 7)
- Pays: 7:6
- House Edge: 1.5 percent
- Means: To make a wager directly on the numbers 6 and/or 8 by what is called a "Place Bet." To do this, you toss your money to the dealer and say something like: "Place the 6 and 8," or just the 6, or just the 8, if that's all you want.

These place bets can be made on all of the box numbers 4, 5, 6, 8, 9, and 10, and can be so placed at any time. Traditionally, they are "off," or "not working," on the come out roll, although it is at your discretion if you so want them. Placing the numbers is a means of getting action on them immediately, without needing them to be rolled twice to gain a win, as would be the case with a come bet that landed on either of these two numbers (or on whatever numbers may be so rolled, or so placed).

Placing the 6 and 8 is one of the best bets in Craps, and a much better method of playing the 6 and 8 directly than to play the Big 6 and Big 8, which are the same bets but carry no odds and offer the house the huge edge of 9.09 percent. A place bet on 6 and/or 8 stays in action until it is won, lost, taken down, or called "off." It is the same bet as for the Big 6 and Big 8, but is paid off at odds, while the other is only paid at even money. Therefore, this is a much better way to wager on the numbers 6 and/or 8. Any Craps player who is making wagers on the Big 6 and Big 8, instead of *placing* the 6 and/or 8, is a fool. Everyone who knows anything about Craps will laugh when they see these silly bets made. The bets on the Big 6 and Big 8 are so bad that many casinos have removed them from the table layout altogether. It's always a sad thing to see anyone making bets on the Big 6 or Big 8, because it's clear that this player knows nothing about the game, and could be making the same bet at odds, and therefore a much better payoff, by simply placing the 6 and/or 8 at the house edge of only 1.5 percent.

Placing the 6 and 8 should always be done in increments of $6, so that you will gain the best payoff, since the pays are 7:6. You won't be able to place odds on this wager, but you can bet in multiples of $6, for wagers of $12, or $24, or $36, or $48, and so on. This also applies to any All Across bets, where the numbers 6 and/or 8 figure in the spread (at least one of them always will).

- What: Place Bet on 5 or 9 (that they *will* be rolled before a 7)
- Pays: 3:2
- House Edge: 4 percent
- Means: To make a place bet on the numbers 5 and/or 9. This is done in exactly the same manner as for all place bets, as described immediately above for the 6 and the 8. All place bets work in the same way. The only difference is the payoffs. The bet stays in action until it is won, lost, taken down, or called "off."

- What: Place Bet on 4 or 10 (that they *will* be rolled before a 7)
- Pays: 2:1
- House Edge: 6.67 percent
- Means: To make a wager on the numbers 4 or 10, similar to the placing of the 6 and the 8, or the 5 and the 9, whereby the bet wins if the 4—or the 10 (if wagered)—is rolled before any 7. The bet stays in action until it is won, lost, taken down, or called "off."

- What: Lay Bet on 6 or 8 (that they *will not* be rolled before a 7)
- Pays: 5:6
- House Edge: 4.1 percent
- Means: The exact *opposite* to placing the 6 and/or the 8. This is the "don't" side.

- What: Lay Bet on 5 or 9 (that they *will not* be rolled before a 7)
- Pays: 2:3
- House Edge: 3.2 percent
- Means: The exact *opposite* to placing the 5 and/or the 9. This is the "don't" side.

- What: Lay Bet on 4 or 10 (that they *will not* be rolled before a 7)
- Pays: 1:2
- House Edge: 2.4 percent
- Means: The exact *opposite* to placing the 4 and/or the 10. This is the "don't" side.

- What: Buy Bet on 6 or 8 (that they *will* be rolled before a 7)
- Pays: 6:5 (less 5 percent commission)
- House Edge: 4.8 percent
- Means: To make a wager on the box numbers of 6 and/or the 8, which is the same kind of a wager as if this were a place bet, except that you are now *buying* the number. This means you are asking the house to pay you at the true odds, rather than at the shaved house odds of the place and/or come bet, on these numbers. Because the house would not be assured of a profit by offering these true-odds payoffs, you will be charged a 5 percent commission. Therefore, to diminish your exposure to that commission, you should push the house to take as high a buy bet as possible and still keep the commission to the nearest whole dollar. For example, the buy bets of 4 and 10—discussed below— are often made at $25 increments, because this will still only cost you a $1 commission, as would be the case with the $20 bet (5 percent of $20 = $1). So, by pushing the house into accepting higher wagers, but still charging only the base commission, you are reducing the house edge on these bets. More on this later.

However, buying the 6 or the 8 is not a good idea. They are much better as place bets instead, because then the house edge is only 1.5 percent; buying the same numbers exposes you to a 4.8 percent house edge.

- What: Buy Bet on 5 or 9 (that they *will* be rolled before a 7)
- Pays: 3:2 (less 5 percent commission)
- House Edge: 4.8 percent
- Means: Same principle as with the above 6 and/or 8

buy bets. Buy bets can be made at any time, although you traditionally would make them only after the come out roll, after the point has been established. They all are done in exactly the same way: Toss your money to the dealer and yell, "Buy the—" and then the number and the amount of your buy bet.

Buying the 5 or the 9 is also not a good idea, for the same reasons as above. Although neither buying nor placing these numbers will put them in the "good" bets category, since they still face a fairly high house edge, by placing the 5 and the 9 instead of buying them, you will expose yourself to a slightly lower house edge. The house edge on these numbers as *place* bets is only 4 percent, while these same bets as *buy* bets expose you to a 4.8 percent house edge.

- What: Buy Bet on 4 or 10 (that they *will* be rolled before a 7)
- Pays: 2:1 (less 5 percent commission)
- House Edge: 4.8 percent
- Means: The same thing as all the buy bets. However,

here is where we can improve our odds, by reducing the house edge. For a $20 bet on either the 4 or the 10, we will be charged a 5 percent commission, or $1. But what if we make a $25 bet? Well, the casinos will not use quarters, to make the commission $1.25, so we get away with making this bet for the $1 commission. This reduces the house edge from 4.8 percent to about 3.84 percent. But what if you push it still further, and buy the 4 and/or 10 for $38? If you can get away with this, then you get the house edge down to almost 2.5 percent, and still pay only the $1 commission.

These are "house pusher" bets, as I call them, because you are forcing the house to take less for more, and pay off at true odds. More on this later, but remember that a house edge of even as low as 2.5 percent on these bets is still a lot more than the average 0.65 percent on a pass line, or come, bets with double odds.

For now, it is worth your while to remember that only the 4 and the 10 are candidates for a buy bet, and conversely *never* a candidate for a place bet. As a place bet, these numbers face the house edge of 6.67 percent. As a buy bet for the correct $20, with the $1 commission, the house edge is only 4.8 percent, much lower than the place bet alternative. By buying the 4 and the 10 for at least $25 each, or more, you will shave the house edge down to around 2.8 percent, which is much lower then the place bet's 6.67 percent. That's why the "all across" bet is never a good idea, because it exposes all your money to these two numbers as place bets, at the high house edge. Instead, there is the place-and-buy alternative, which you can learn in Chapter Seven.

Well, that's it. Now you know what pays what, what it means, how it's done, what the house edge is, and what the true odds really are on some of those ugly house bets. This is what you should know about Craps "by the numbers."

Some of the bets shown above are among the best bets in the casino, while others are among the worst. A standard line bet with double odds, for example, reduces the house edge to about 0.65 percent, and this can be pushed even lower by the availability of higher free odds. Among all the house-banked games, only Blackjack and Baccarat can be as good. In Baccarat, you are facing a house edge of about 1.1 percent on the "bank" bets and about 1.4 percent on the "player" bets. Pretty good, but Craps is better. Pass line and come bets with double odds both beat this to a pulp. Blackjack is a game where the average Basic Strategy player can reduce the expected house edge to about 0.5 percent, and almost to 0.1 percent on some games, when using a progressive betting strategy (please refer to my book *Powerful Profits from Blackjack* for more details). More advanced players can swing this into a player-positive expectation game.

Craps cannot become a statistically player-positive expectation game, because the best bets can only reduce the house edge to 0.02 percent, as in the case of 100x odds. The game is still a "house game," by definition. This simply means that, over the life span of the Craps table's events, the house will always get that percentage of "wins" on those events as wagered, in accordance with the percentages inherent in the game. For this reason, Craps is still a game that cannot be beaten, at least not statistically, over the long-term events. However, this does not mean that it should not be played. Quite the contrary. Even slot machines, which are most definitely a "house game" because they hold a steady percentage for the house, have to pay off. Otherwise, no one would play them (for more information on Slots, please read my book, *Powerful Profits from Slots*).

Craps is among the elite groups of casino table games where players playing correctly can gain a game whose inherent house withholding percentages are nearly "zero," statistically speaking. Even the most novice of all Craps players can immediately enter into this game with a Three Bet Plan, which I will discuss later, and start playing with a house edge *below* one percent. For these reasons, Craps is among the best games in the casino. Sadly, it has been passed by and mostly misunderstood by the newer generations of casino players, who are more used to electronic gambling games. Let's hope we can change that here, and offer you an introduction into the game of Craps that will show you how this can be a pleasurable and profitable game.

Introduction to Craps

This chapter is designed to provide every reader with an overview of the game of casino Craps, as the game is now being played in the casinos in the United States. Although some of the information in this chapter repeats information presented in the previous chapter, this cannot be changed because "Craps by the numbers" is what this game is about. Therefore, to prepare you for this chapter, it was necessary to explain all the "numbers" knowledge. Now, in this chapter, I can begin the process of "demystifying" the game of Craps, with the intent to show that it is an easy game to learn and to play.

While I also recognize that many readers may have purchased this book because they are already familiar with Craps, but wanted to gain an insight into some of the better methods of maximizing profitability, I would like to welcome even these experienced players into the world of the simplified game of Craps. Perhaps you may be able to find something in these words that you may not have thought of before. If you are an experienced Craps player, I still hope you will read these introductory pages, where I lay the foundation for Craps playing strategies that exploit, and explore, the best methods and means of making powerful profits from this game.

Those of you who have bought this book because you were looking for a simple explanation of the game, and a quick introduction into how to play it well—and profitably—will also find this section of value. Here, I take a little more time to show the real simplicity of the game. Although Craps may look very confusing, especially to those who previously have not been exposed to it, or have wanted to play the game but were afraid to, I absolutely wish to let you know that such fears are unfounded. This is a terrific game, with several very good value bets available. I therefore begin by showing you that Craps can be as easy as an "either-or" situation.

A SIMPLE GAME

Craps *looks* like a very complicated game, and indeed it can be if you decide to delve into the many different betting options that are available. However, as you will shortly find out, the game can also be as *simple as you want to make it*.

At its simplest, Craps offers two basic choices:

One: You can bet that the shooter **will win**; or
Two: You can bet that the shooter **will not** win.

That's it. Other nuances of the game are described below.

How Craps Is Played

The casino game of Craps is played with a set of two perfectly balanced dice, usually red in color, each with six faces numbered 1 through 6 by means of white dots. The game is played by tossing both dice from one of the narrow ends of the table to the other, making sure that both dice hit the opposite side wall of the table. The inside walls of the table are covered with a kind of serrated egg-carton rubberized foam, designed to make the dice bounce around to ensure randomness.

Each throw of the dice is called a "roll." Players take turns rolling the dice, clockwise around the table, and the player rolling at any given time is called the "shooter." When a new shooter is given the dice, his or her first roll is called the "come out" roll. This begins a new series of rolls by that shooter, and lasts for as long as that shooter continues to make winning rolls. Payoffs are made based on the number combination displayed when the dice come to rest.

A "new game" in Craps begins with the come out roll. A come out roll can be made only if either the table is empty and a new player, or players, just walk up; or, if the game is already in progress, the current shooter fails to make a winning roll—more correctly known as "not making the point," or "seven out." A new game then begins with a new shooter. If the current shooter *does* make his point, the dice are returned to him and he then begins the new come out roll. This is a continuation of that shooter's roll, although, technically, the come out roll identifies a new game about to begin.

When the shooter fails to make his point, the dice are then offered to the next player for a new come out roll, and the game continues in the same manner. The new shooter will be the person directly to the left of the previous shooter. This person could be you right away, or not, depending on

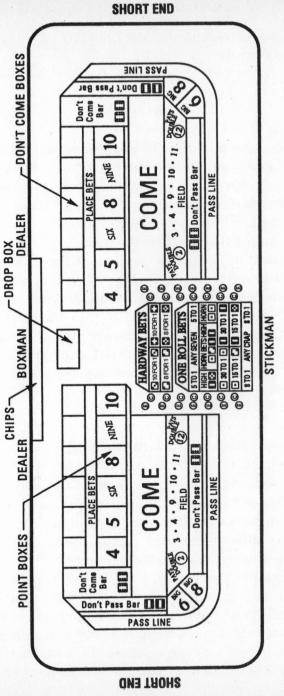

A standard Craps table layout.

33

which position (around the table) the dice are in when you come into the game.

The Puck

It now becomes important to mention a device that looks like a hockey puck, called "the puck," or sometimes "the buck." It is white on one side and black on the other, and is used by the dealers to identify the "point." Once the point is established by the shooter, the dealer will move this puck to that point number and turn the white side up.

The puck stays on this point until the shooter either makes his point or he sevens out. When this happens the puck is moved to the *don't-come-bar-12* area, and turned black side up. The significance of this device is only in tracking the game. White side up over a point indicates the game is in progress and that this box number is the point. Black side up means a new come out roll is about to take place.

WHAT WINS AND WHAT LOSES

In Craps, winning or losing depends on a variety of different possible outcomes of any roll of the two dice, and on which of these possibilities you bet. The two dice can produce many different number combinations. Some can be made several ways, others only one way.

For example, the number 6 can be rolled by two dice as follows: 5, 1; 4, 2; 3+3; 2, 4; and 1, 5. But the number 2 can only be rolled one way: 1+1. Numbers such as 6, which can be rolled several ways, don't pay as much as numbers that can be rolled only one way—unless you are betting that the number will be rolled in a specific way, such has 3+3, known as *Hardways.* All winning payoffs are, therefore, determined by the frequency in which any two-dice number combinations can be rolled. Generally, the harder the combination is to roll, the more it will pay, and vice versa.

On the come out roll, the pass line bet wins if the shooter rolls a 7 or an 11. The bet loses automatically if the shooter rolls 2, 3, or 12. This is known as "rolling craps." If the shooter rolls either 4, 5, 6, 8, 9, or 10, winning your bet now depends on whether the shooter will roll this same number again *before rolling any 7.* Otherwise, the pass line bets lose.

Rolling any of these numbers—4, 5, 6, 8, 9, or 10 (called "box numbers")—*on the come out roll* is called "establishing the point." Any number so rolled is thereafter referred to as the "point." Establishing a point is an event that happens as the immediate result of the come out roll, unless that come out roll results in 7, 11, 2, 3, or 12, in which case more rolls must be made until a point is established.

Although taking advantage of the many betting options can involve a considerable degree of mastery, in its simplest form Craps is a game where players bet either that the shooter *will* make winning rolls, or that he or she *will not* make winning rolls.

Betting that the shooter *will* make winning rolls is called betting "with the shooter" (also called "betting right"). Betting that the shooter *will not* make winning rolls is called "betting against the shooter" (also called "betting wrong"). There is nothing "right" or "wrong" with either of these bets— they are simply called that.

Betting *with* the Shooter

To bet with the shooter, you place your bet in an area marked "pass line," which is known as making a "line bet."

This so-called *pass line* is a strip on the table layout marked by two lines roughly two inches wide that rim the entire table layout across from the "boxman." Bets *with* the shooter win if the shooter either rolls a 7 or an 11 on the come out roll or makes the point, and lose if the shooter rolls "craps" on the come out roll or rolls any 7 *before* making the point.

Betting *Against* the Shooter

To bet against the shooter, you place your bet in an area marked "don't pass." This area is also a strip on the table layout, and it rims the table directly above the pass line. This bet is almost the *exact opposite* to the pass line bet (since the 12 is a push on the "don't"), and wins if the shooter rolls either "any craps" on the come out roll, or rolls any 7 *before* rolling the point number. "Don't pass" bets *lose* otherwise, which means that the *pass line bets won.* Therefore, the "don't" side is the direct *opposite* to the front line.

HOW TO BEGIN

As with all table games, you begin by changing your cash money into gaming chips. In Craps you do this by throwing your money on the table and asking for "change." If the table is playing "well" there will be a lot of people crowding around and a lot of noise, so make sure you speak up! Also, it is a good idea—as well as a courtesy to other players—to wait and ask for change *between* rolls of the dice.

No matter what stage the game is in, whether on the come out roll or in progress, you can jump in immediately and place any bets. The only exception to this is the bet called the "pass line bet *with odds*," which can be made *only on the come out roll* (a pass line bet first, and then—after the point has been established—placing the "odds" bet behind it). You can, however, bet *with* the shooter even while the game is in progress, by placing a pass line bet *without odds.* This is done by placing your gaming chips halfway over one of the two lines framing the pass line area—the line nearest to you. It is, however, an inadvisable bet, because after the point has been established, the front line player faces a statistical disadvantage. There are several casinos that will actually allow you to make a pass line bet *with* odds after the point is established. This is called a "put bet." If the point is 6 or 8, the put-plus-6 or 8 with odds is as good as a place bet on 6 or 8; with less odds (lower than on the place bet) this bet is a little worse, while with more odds it gets better. Nevertheless, for simplicity's sake, it will be easier for you to remember that in most casinos the pass line bet after the point has been established will traditionally be allowed only *without* free odds. Also, to make a pass line bet *after* the point has been established means that you will be giving up the best part of the pass line bet, which is the come out roll, where you have 8 ways to win and only 4 ways to lose. It's just not a good bet, regardless of what the "finer" points in betting may be.

Before the new shooter rolls the dice on his or her come out roll, a variety of bets can be made. The easiest and most common are the above-mentioned pass line and don't pass line bet. But after a point is established by the shooter, you can then place an additional bet behind your pass line bet. This is called "taking odds."

In most casinos you can bet up to *double* the amount of your *pass line* bet. This is called "taking full odds." Some casinos offer up to 10x odds; this simply means that you can bet up to 10 times the amount of your pass line bet once a point is established (3x odds or 5x odds in some casinos, or even up to 100x odds, but it all means the same—only the amounts of your maximum-odds bets are affected by whatever these limits at such casinos are; for the sake of simplicity, I will mostly use the example of the 2*x* odds, often called "double odds" or "full odds").

Betting the *don't pass* line is *almost* the *exact opposite* of betting the pass line. If you do this on the come out roll, your don't pass bet *wins* if the shooter rolls any "craps"—2 or 3 (ties on 12)—and *loses automatically* on any 7 and 11. Tying on 12 simply means that there is no decision—your don't pass bet neither wins nor loses, merely stays in limbo till a decision is reached on subsequent rolls.

If the shooter establishes a point, your don't pass bet stays in action, but to win your bet the shooter must roll a 7 before making his point. Therefore, a don't pass bet *wins* if the shooter *fails* to make his point, but *loses* if the shooter *does* make the point. You can also lay odds on a don't pass bet.

A *don't pass* bet is not a bad bet, but I will not recommend it for the casual player since some of the requirements can be a little too complex, at least conceptually. Betting *with the shooter* is a far easier method to grasp in a short time, and offers many more advantages. The wrong-way wagers require you to bet more to win less. Although these may be good bets in some circumstances, I just don't like the "dark side," and so most of my discussions, at least in this chapter, will be for bets *with* the shooter.

BETTING OPTIONS

The complexity in Craps is only due to the many *betting options* that the player can make. Of all the table games available in casinos, Craps offers the most player choices, and is therefore the game of preference among serious gamblers. It also provides some good odds, and it is very possible to make lots of money very quickly when playing it. Because this is very important, I will say it again: Players begin by making two choices:

One: Bet the "pass" line; or
Two: Bet the "don't pass" line.

Betting the pass line means that you are betting *with* the shooter, and by so doing you wager that he will either make a 7 or an 11 on his come out roll; that he *will not* roll any craps; that he *will roll a point* (if he doesn't roll either 7, 11, or any craps), and that eventually he *will roll his point number again* before rolling a 7, after first establishing the point.

The don't pass line is almost exactly the opposite of the pass line. (Remember that pesky push on the 12.) If you bet this you are betting *against* the shooter, and *betting on almost exactly the opposite outcome to any pass line bets.* In this case you *want* the shooter to roll any craps, or *fail* to make his point after establishing it.

Most players will bet the pass line, and go *with* the shooter. But betting against the shooter is also a good bet, especially if the dice are "cold," meaning shooters are not making points and are "crapping out" a lot. Many regular Craps players will tell you to bet the don't pass line if you are betting from 3 A.M. to 10 A.M. This is known as the "graveyard shift," and Craps players will tell you this is because of the numerous pass line bettors who have been "buried" during these hours. The basis for this superstition is that the dice are "cold" because at 3 A.M. casinos change the dice and introduce new, fresh, unplayed dice. There is something to be said for this superstition. New dice have all sharp corners, they have not been played, and their roll nuances are not known. Since Craps is a streaky game, Craps players tend to watch for short-term trends in dice rolls. New dice are therefore unpredictable. And since they are

new, their newness also means that they have as yet not
"worn down"—even if only slightly—through heavy play.
Craps players like to play "hot" dice, meaning dice that
have been in action for some time. So, if you find yourself
playing Craps in the wee hours of the morning, Craps players will almost unanimously advise you to bet *against* the
shooter, even if the shooter is yourself!

However this does not mean that *all* games at those hours
will be so cold. Some casinos, especially during weekends
and holidays, run hot Craps action throughout the night,
and on those occasions the dice may remain hot. It's a matter of choice for the player, based on knowledge and observation of the game.

The Smart Play

Normally, the smart play for a casual Craps player is to bet
the pass line, *with* the shooter, and *take full odds.*

To bet the pass line means you place a bet on the line
marked as "pass." You can bet any amount of money from
the table minimum, usually $5, up to the table maximum,
usually $5,000 on a $5 minimum table. Other limits apply
from $1 minimum bet tables to $500 minimum bet tables,
depending on the game limits. But most casual players will
take advantage of the $5 minimum tables.

You place your bet on the pass line and wait for the roll.
If the shooter rolls either a 7 or an 11, you automatically
win even money, and the game begins over again with the
same shooter. If the shooter rolls any Craps, 2, 3, or 12, you
automatically lose your bet, and the game begins over again,
still with the same shooter.

If the shooter rolls 4, 5, 6, 8, 9, or 10 (called "box numbers"), this is called "establishing the point." If you bet the
pass line, winning your bet now depends on whether the

shooter will roll *this same number again* before rolling any 7. This is called "making the point." If the shooter rolls any 7 before making his point, all pass line bets and odds lose; all point bets and odds lose; come bets win even money; and don't pass and don't come bets win (amounts depend on numbers bet and odds taken).

If the shooter *does* make his point, all pass line bets and odds win; come bets are placed on the point; point bets ride unless called off; and all don't come and don't pass bets lose. Again, the exact opposite to pass line bets.

Taking Odds

If the shooter establishes a point, and you think he *will* make the point, you can place odds on your pass line bet. Many casinos offer double odds, triple odds, even 10x odds or more. Taking odds means placing more money *behind* your pass line bet.

You can take single odds, meaning you place an extra $5 behind your $5 pass line bet, or double odds, meaning you place $10 behind your pass line bet, unless the point is 6 or 8, in which case you can place $15 for double odds, and so on for the odds scale, depending on the casino.

Some casinos will let you push this as much as the odds allow, and even tell you to make the proper-size odds bet. Others may not tell you straight out, but the dealers will if you ask them. At other casinos, depending on the jurisdiction, they may not allow you to do this at all. Basically, you are adding more money to your odds bet on the 6 and the 8 as the point, or come, because you are getting a 6:5 payoff. As a place bet, the 6 and the 8 should always be bet in multiples of $6. But if you make a line bet of $5, and the point is either 6 or 8, or you land on the 6 and/or the 8 through the come bet, your "double odds" free odds bet should be $12. Most casinos don't like fractions, as we will shortly find out on the buy bets. So, in these cases, many casinos will actually allow you to take a $15 free odds bet to keep payoffs easier to calculate, thus making the game faster (as well as encouraging you to bet more, of course). It is, however, in your interest to do this, because you will be paid closest to the true odds for these two numbers by incrementally pushing your odds bet as high as the house will allow. Of course, if the house allows more than double odds, then you can't push the house on the front line in this manner. However, you can still take advantage of the payoffs by graduating your odds.

These are called "free odds," because they are paid at true odds. This "odds" bet then rides on the outcome of the game, along with your pass line bet. By making this bet you are betting that the shooter *will* make his point. Taking full odds (maximum odds offered by that casino) also reduces the overall in-built house edge on these bets, and makes it statistically more advantageous for the player. You also have the added benefit that the free odds carry no house edge.

If the shooter makes the point, all pass line bets and odds are paid, as well as other appropriate bets, and the dice go back to the same shooter for a new come out roll. The way to tell this from watching the game is to watch the "puck" being moved around by the dealers.

Once the shooter establishes a point, the game can go on for some time even if the shooter does not make the point right away. This is called "rolling the numbers." What this means is that this shooter is very lucky and is rolling lots of numbers *other than 7*. If this happens players usually make lots of money betting the come bets and taking odds on their come bet numbers, or placing or buying numbers. Such a roll is most definitely a *hot roll*.

Come Bets

When a hot roll on box numbers starts to happen—in fact, at any time after a point has been established—in addition to your pass line bet and odds you can also put a bet in the "come" area. This "come" bet wins even money if the shooter should roll a 7 at that time, but your pass line bet and odds lose, so you don't want to bet it for that reason. But this bet can also win even money if the shooter rolls an 11, in which case you don't lose your pass line bet and odds, and the game goes on.

If the shooter is rolling numbers, you should bet the come bet so that you get on some of the numbers the shooter is rolling. When you place your come bet, and the shooter rolls, say, a 5, with the point being, say, 8, the dealer will put your money on the number 5.

This number then plays in the same manner as your pass line bet. You can take odds on that number the same as on the pass line bet. Winning this bet depends on whether the shooter will roll the number 5 *again* and *before* rolling a 7. If he does, the dealer will take the bet down, pay you, and you collect your money. Then you can do this again. You can make come bets continuously throughout that shooter's roll, as many times as you like. If you already have all the numbers covered and you make another come bet, and it wins, the dealer will simply pay you that number's win and odds on the come bet. You can do this again and again. It all depends on how long you think that particular shooter can roll numbers before rolling a 7. In effect, making a come bet, or placing or buying numbers, plays in the same manner as a pass line bet. They pay off when hit *before* the shooter rolls a 7, and *lose otherwise,* unless the shooter makes his point, in which case they ride on the come out roll unless you call them off, or take them "down."

"Off"—"Down"—"Working" Bets

If you call your bets "off," the dealer will place a small marker over your numbers with the word "off" on it, signifying that although your money is still on the table it is "not in action," meaning not at risk. In effect, it is as if the money isn't there at all. But it remains yours.

If you call your numbers "down" (other than the original pass line and the original come bets, which cannot be so called down) by saying "down on all my numbers," the dealer will pick up all your bets and give them to you and you can start all over on the next roll or game. Calling your bets "down" is usually done if you placed or bought the numbers, or made proposition bets. If you have pass line or don't pass odds, you can pick them up, but not the original bet. If you have come bets, you can take your odds "down," but not your original bets.

After the point has been established, the don't pass and don't come bets and odds *can* be taken down because now the player has the statistical edge, and therefore the casino will gladly let you take your bets down if you want. You will, however, be better advised not to do so. If you don't like the way this roll is going, you could just call them "off" instead.

You do not have to call *all* your numbers "down"—you can call any one, or more, of your numbers "down" and keep some others in action, or, if you want, call all your numbers "down," depending on what you want to do.

Calling "off" has the same effect as calling "down," except that calling "off" means your money stays on the table until you say "working," meaning you want this money back in action on those same numbers, or call them "down."

Calling them "down" means you get all your money back (except original line bets and come bets), but you must start all over again after the next point is established. In most cases it is better to call the numbers "off," and then simply put them back in the action when you so want, by calling "working."

But if the point *was made,* if you don't call your *come bets, place* or *buy bets* "off," they will ride on the new come out roll. If a 7 is rolled, your new pass line bet wins, your "riding" come bets from the previous roll lose, and your come bet odds are returned to you. On the come out roll it's always a good thing to call your bets off, particularly any of your proposition bets. However, it may be worthwhile for you to keep your come bets working, depending on how you want to play, how the table has been playing, and what you think the next shooter is likely to roll. But if you do you're risking *all* the original bets, including the free odds. More on this later.

Place and Buy

You can also *place* or *buy* the numbers. This is similar to the come bet, except you simply tell the dealer which number or numbers you want your money on and give him your base bet amount and odds; he will put it on the number or numbers you ask for. Instead of waiting for the shooter to roll that number and then to roll it again before any 7 for you to win—as in the case of a *come* bet—you are now simply betting that the shooter will roll that number at least once, *before* he rolls a 7.

For example, toss out $15 and call out: "On the 9." This means you are telling the dealer that this money is to go directly on the number 9, without you first making a come bet, then waiting for the 9 to be rolled, then placing the odds, and then waiting for the 9 to be rolled again before any 7. Any number so placed then plays the same as if it was achieved by making a come bet, except that you can call the whole bet "down," which you could not do with your come bet. If you landed on this number through the come bet, then only your free odds can be taken "down." If you make this a place bet instead, then the entire wager can be called "down" at any time. However, the payoffs are different, so take a look at Chapter One for each of the box numbers and what they pay as come bets, versus place bets. Also, it is important for you to remember that unless you call out "buy," any bet you toss out to the dealer and ask to be put on any specified number will *automatically* be put as a "place" bet. Therefore, if you want to "buy" the number instead of "placing" it, you must say the words—for example: "Buy the 9 for twenty dollars," or whatever the number, or amount you are wagering, may be. You should remember, however, that if you "buy" a number, the casino will charge you a 5 percent commission. This is so because payoffs in these betting events are paid at true odds.

The advantage of placing or buying numbers is that you can immediately cover all the available numbers, in addition to the shooter's point, and don't have to wait for the shooter to roll that number first and then roll it again—as in a come bet. But you can only do this *after* the point is established.

To cover *all* the box numbers with a "place" bet, you simply call out "all across." This means that you have chosen to bet on *all the box numbers* in addition to whatever box number is the point. On a $5 minimum table "all across" will cost you $27, unless the point is 6 or 8, in which case this bet will cost you $26. You can bet this up to the table maximum in equal increments of $27 or $26 ($5 on 4, 5, 9, and 10, and $6 each on 6 and 8, allowing for whatever point has been established).

The advantage in "buying" numbers is that winners are paid at *true odds,* but you have to pay your bet commission up front (some casinos may allow you to pay the vig only on the win; this is an advantage to you, and you should always ask about it; more on this later). You can also only do this *after* the shooter has established his point. To "buy" a number you must tell the dealer this is a "buy bet." You can do this, for example, by saying: "Buy the 10 for $25."

Whether you made a come bet or placed numbers, whatever number or numbers you have selected play in addition to the point number. If, as in my earlier example, you had the number 5, and the point was 8, you want the shooter to roll a 5 *and/or* an 8. Either way, you win. If he rolls a 5 first, and then an 8, so much the better. That's a hot roll and that's how you can make a lot of money fast.

For the "don't pass" and "don't come" bets, remember that they are *exactly the opposite* to what I have just outlined. Whatever wins on the "don't pass" and "don't come" bets would lose on the pass line or come bets or place bets, and vice versa.

If you come into a game in progress and you see that the shooter is hot, you are better off making come bets, or placing or buying the numbers. And if the shooter continues to roll hot, you may then consider making the pass line bet, because, the way this shooter is going, he is likely to make his point, or pass, on the come out roll—meaning a winning roll of 7 or 11.

Watching the Roll

Craps is a very subjective game; no two players will play it the same way, even if both have the same level of knowledge and expertise. Because of the many choices possible in this game, players tend to focus on certain patterns of betting behavior, and modify this betting behavior only in accordance with how the shooters are rolling.

If your tendency is to bet *with* the shooter, you will most likely not change your betting behavior and start betting against the shooter if he is running cold. Most players will simply ease off on their pass line bets, lay off the numbers, and sit back and wait for a "hot turn" (a new shooter who can warm up the dice).

This kind of subjective betting behavior can be a killer in Blackjack, but not necessarily in Craps. Craps offers so many possibilities for the players that even players with very limited knowledge of the game, and many bad betting habits, can come out ahead.

As with all gambling, the keys to success are basic knowledge, a good bankroll, some luck, and simply keeping your eyes open, all of which will give you ammunition for more informed choices. This is true especially in Craps, because in this game if you see a pattern emerge, bet into it. This is the "hot roll" we all look for.

Hardways

When betting Hardways you are betting that the shooter will roll 4, 6, 8, or 10 in *paired combinations*: 2+2, 3+3, 4+4 or 5+5. You can make this bet on just one of these possibilities—say, "hard 4"—or two, three, or all four of them. These bets then ride until the shooter either rolls one of these numbers in the "hard" way combination, or rolls that number "easy," or until you call these bets "off" or "down," or the shooter craps out—in which case all your Hardways still in action lose.

To roll a Hardways number "easy" means that the number was rolled in a combination *other than* a Hardways pair. For instance, a "hard 6" means that the shooter has to roll a two-die combination of 6 exactly as 3+3. If the shooter rolls this combination *in any other way,* say 5+1, this is called "6 easy." In this event your Hardways 6 will lose. If your Hardways number is rolled the "hard" way, you get paid: 8 for 1 on the 4 and 10 (7:1), and 10 for 1 on the 6 and 8 (9:1).

If the shooter makes the point, the Hardways bets stay in action for the next roll, the come out roll, but will lose if the next roll is a 7 or 11, or if the shooter rolls the number easy. Therefore, you can protect your Hardways bets until the next point is established by either asking for "Hardways down," which means the dealer will pick up your money and give it back to you; or you can call them "off" for the come out roll by saying, "Hardways off." If you call "Hardways off" and the new point is established, you can then call "Hardways working" and all subsequent rolls will have your hardways bets in play again.

Most of the time the dealer will automatically call out, "Hardways working unless called off," or simply ask you if you want your Hardways to work on the come out roll. You then tell him "Hardways off on the come out" if you want the Hardways off, or you can call "working," in which case the bets ride. It is also good to remember that you can call your Hardways off at any time during the roll for as long as you want. To do this you just call them "off" in the same way you would had this been a come out roll. And to get the bets in action again at any time after you called them off, you just say "working."

This method of calling your bets "off" and "working" really does not help a great deal, especially if you are a novice player. Often, people who fancy themselves as experts at the game call their bets off and on throughout the game for no apparent reason. This tends to infuriate the dealers, but don't be concerned with what the dealers feel. Remember that *you* are the customer, so if that's how you want to play, play that way. However, calling your Hardways or come bets off and on during the game is an exercise in guesswork. Sometimes you can guess right, and sometimes wrong. The best policy is to let it stay in action if you bet it, and take your chances with the roll. The *only* time it pays to call your bets off is *on the come out roll,* and that is because your Hardways bets can lose automatically if the shooter rolls 7 or 11, or if any of your Hardways bets are rolled "easy." Not a good deal.

If you want to make a hardway bet, you toss whatever amount of money you want to bet to the stickman at the center of the table and call out your bet, say, "Hard 6." The stickman will then put that amount of your money on that hardway bet. If you want to cover all the Hardways, you select how much you want on each of the four possible hardway numbers, and then call out, say, "All the Hardways, $5 each." This means you toss $20 on the table and the Stickman will place $5 on each of the four Hardways numbers.

At any time during the game if one of your Hardways is rolled easy, the Stickman will call something like, "Easy 6, six easy, hard 6 down." This means you lost your bet on the hard 6, but your other three numbers are still in play. Most of the time if the dealers and Stickman know you are betting Hardways, either one or the other will ask you if you want to "go back up." This means they want to know if you want to replace the bet you just lost. If you do, you just toss in the amount of money you want back on that number, and the game goes on.

At any time during the game if any of your Hardways are rolled the "hard" way, you will be paid as long as you have a bet in action on that hardway number. Also, you have an option to "press" your bet at any time during the game.

TO "PRESS" YOUR BET

To "press" a bet means you want to *increase* the amount of money on that bet, usually done in equal increments. Except for the pass line and don't pass bet, you can "press" *any* bet. In the case of hardway bets, all you have to do is call out, "Press my hard 6," and throw out the amount of money you want that bet to be increased by to the center of the table. This tells the dealers and Stickman that this money is to go on the number you called. It is called a "press" because you are pressing the number with more money, of course with the intent to get a bigger win. This can also be done if your bet won. Instead of accepting the money you just won, you can call out "press it," and the dealer will automatically add the next correct highest amount to the bet that just won. This can be done for any bet, other than the original pass line and don't pass line bets (and, of course, the original come and don't come bets).

Although these bets contain some of the highest house edges, making Hardways bets may be a good idea if you see the shooter roll a lot of paired combinations. Calling your hard bets off, or taking them down, is a good idea on each new come out roll. Pressing your bets is *always* a good idea, especially after a win. When you win on a Hardways bet, or on a number bet, pressing it the same amount of money will give you double the action with *only your original bet at risk*. This is the best way to make some good money in Craps. If you press and hit, take the win; then if you hit again, press again, and so on. When you lose, go back to your original bet. This is a very simple "strategy" at best, but it helps to show a quick way to make some great money quickly, with only the original bet at risk (meaning if you lose, you stand to lose only the first bet you made, while you stand to win twice, or more, that amount if you hit after having pressed the bet; more on this later).

Field Bets

Most action in Craps takes place on the pass line, don't pass line, come, and the box numbers. In addition, players can make *one-roll* bets on a variety of possible outcomes of the next roll. These are called "proposition" bets. Field bets are one such option.

To make a field bet you simply put your money in the area marked "Field." Again, you can bet from the table minimum up to the table maximum. Such table limits are universal for all action on that table. When you make a field bet you are betting that *on the next roll* the shooter will roll any one of the field numbers: 2, 3, 4, 5, 9, 10, 11, or 12. If the shooter rolls any of these numbers, you win. Number 2 and number 12 pay 2:1, all other field bets pay even money (in some casinos, 2 and 12 will pay a bonus, or pay 3:1).

If the shooter rolls *any other number,* these bets lose. Remember, these are *one-roll bets* only; therefore each subsequent roll of the dice is a new game for these field bets, as with all other one-roll bets, and if you want to play them again you have to make a new bet each time.

Other One-Roll Bets

In addition to field bets, players can wager on: "any craps," "snake eyes," "box cars," "ace-deuce," "Yo-eleven," "any-seven," and "Horn." All of these have been explained in Chapter One, so check back to see what they are, and what they pay.

None of these bets are in action very much, and there's a good reason for it. These are one-roll, one-result bets, with an extremely high edge *favoring the house,* and are not rolled often enough to warrant the expenditure relative to potential win—especially when the other aspects of the game offer so much better odds of winning overall and so many more favorable choices and betting combinations for the players.

Come Bets

I have already discussed come bets to some extent, so here is a recap with some additional information.

A come bet is a bet placed in the area marked "come" and can be made *only after the shooter has established his point.* Let's say the shooter established 5 as his point. You can then make a come bet, and you decide to put $5 in the "come" area. The shooter then rolls again and rolls, say, 9. The $5 chip you placed in the "come" area is now picked up by the dealer and put on the number 9. You can now take odds on your "come-9," as this bet is now called. In this example you are betting that the shooter will again roll a 9 before he rolls a 7. So, if you also bet the pass line, you now have two bets in play: your pass line bet (which plays on the point—the 5), and the 9 (which is your come number).

If the shooter makes the point before he rolls your 9, your pass line bet wins and your come bet on the 9 rides for the next roll, the come out roll, unless you call it off or take it down (the only time you can take your *entire* come bet "down"—in addition to the odds—is after the point is made and before the next come out roll). If the shooter *does* roll your 9 *before* he rolls a 7, you win. The dealer will now pay you for your bet plus odds (if you took odds, which you should always do) and put the money in front of you. You then have to pick it up. If you don't, the money will ride as a come bet on the next roll. Remember, you're in control, so you have to pick up your winnings, make your bets, and always tell the dealer what you are doing when you put money down.

After you made your first come bet and the come bet went to your 9, as in my example here, you can then make another come bet. If the shooter rolls another 9 right away, the dealer will pay you for your 9 and your come bet goes back on the 9. This is called "off and on." Usually, if this happens, the dealer will simply pay the 9 bet on the come bet area. In this case you should pick up your winnings and leave only the chips you want for the next come bet, if you want to make another come bet. If the shooter rolls another number, say 6, the dealer will take your second come bet and put it on the number 6.

The process then repeats itself. You can take odds on the 6 and the game plays as before. Now you have three bets in play: your pass line bet (which covers the point), your come-9, and your come-6. So, using my example, if the shooter rolls either 6, 9, or 5, you win (considering the 5 the current point for this example).

All come bets automatically lose if the shooter rolls any Craps while the bet is in the "come" area. Once your come bet is on the come number, you can lose this bet only if the shooter rolls a 7 *before* rolling your come number. But you can call this come bet off any time during the game before the shooter rolls a 7, by saying "come bets off." You can also take your odds down, but not the original come bet, except after the point was made and before the next roll.

BIG 6 AND BIG 8

"Big 6" and "Big 8" are even-money bets, and by putting your money on either the Big 6 or the Big 8 you are betting that the shooter will roll either a 6 or an 8 *before* rolling any 7. A really silly bet. These are *prize-sucker* bets, particularly since if you "place" the 6 and/or the 8, you will be paid *with odds,* while a bet on the "bigs" will *only pay even money.*

Why bet this? People do, and the casinos love them because these dummies are losers even if they win. These bets carry the high house edge of 9.09 percent, while the *same bets made as place bets* can reduce the house edge to a mere 1.5 percent.

SIMPLE STRATEGY

Although we will begin our discussion of Craps strategy in Chapter Seven, here is a short introduction to one of the best and *simplest* playing strategies for Craps.

1. *Always bet the pass line.* Start with the table minimum, and if you are winning, press your *odds* bet by one chip each time you have a winner (preferably in correctly structured increments for maximum-odds pay). Go back to the table minimum each time you hit a loser.

2. *Always take full odds* on the pass line or come bets. Most casinos offer double odds, so take them. With a $5 minimum bet, your odds will be an extra $10, so you have $15 riding on each such bet. If you are in a casino that offers triple odds, or 10x odds, start with double odds, and if you're winning, increase your odds proportionately. Most casinos will now offer at least the double odds, so if you start with single odds, and my number one advice calls for increase, you may soon hit the table maximum for odds bets. In this case, start increasing your pass line bets by one chip each time, and so increase your free odds in equivalent increments. This advice applies *only* to those casinos where you cannot increase your free odds bets past double the original wager.

Many casinos, however, will offer more than double odds. Free odds of 3x, 5x, 10x, and 25x odds are common. Some casinos even offer 50x and 100x odds. It is to your advantage to play in casinos that offer the *highest* free odds. If you are in such a casino, *never* increase the front line bet over and above the minimum. If the minimum is a $5 line bet, then only make this; and if you are winning, simply keep increasing the *odds* bets. This is good for you because the original line bet only pays off at 1:1, while facing the house edge of 1.4 percent, while the free odds are paid at true odds and face no house edge. Together, the higher the odds bet you make, the overall lower the house edge on the combined bet will be. So, simply remember that if you are betting the pass line, and come, and you are winning, don't increase the size of your original wager—increase instead the amount of your free odds.

3. *If you are making a come bet, make two.* This way you will have three amounts in action: your pass line bets and odds, and your two come bets and odds. This is a good way to start your play, and won't hurt you too much if you hit a cold table and lose a few turns. (Refer to the Three Bet Plan in Chapter Seven for more details.)

4. If you're feeling good about the shooters on this table, you may consider placing the 6 and the 8 (or the other if one is the point), and buying the 4 and the 10. This will give you action on the point, the 6 and/or the 8, and the 4 and the 10, at the bet odds with the lowest house edge. (Refer to the Four and Six Bet Plans in Chapter Seven for more details.)

5. *Don't bet Field, Big 6, Big 8, Hardways, or any of the other one-roll bets.* Until you know more about this game, these bets can easily eat you up and distract you from making your other bets properly. These are high house edge bets.

6. *Manage your money.* The racks on Craps tables (called "rails") offer an easy way to keep track of your stake and your winnings. Keep an eye out on how much you have. If you are winning, bet more. After all, by that time you are betting with the casino's money. Remember that

only the money you brought with you is at risk. Anything else on top of this is winnings. Divide these winnings into "keep money" and "play money." If you have lots of play money left, bet more. Especially if you hit a lucky shooter and get in at the start of a hot roll.

The desired outcome in Craps, as with any gambling game, is to win. To do this, you, the player, must possess at least some basic information as to how to go about it. The simple strategy I have outlined here will give you the *quickest and best introductory* information for betting choices, and is designed to maximize your winning potential. Even if you visit a casino only once and want to try Craps, by practicing these simple rules you will have a much better chance of winning money than otherwise, and you will certainly enjoy the game more. Craps is a fascinating game and can quickly capture your continued interest. And even if you are already a regular casino visitor and may even have played Craps before, keeping these suggestions in mind will make you a smarter player.

The Good, The Bad, and the Ugly

Chapters One and Two were designed to give you an opportunity to get to know the game of Craps quickly and easily, to provide you with a simple overview of the game, and to show you a betting approach that allows you to go directly to any Craps table and play. If all you wanted to know was what bets do what, what they pay, why, how to make them, what you will be paid, and how to make bets more efficiently, the previous two chapters are all you need. Nevertheless, this is not the whole story. Just because we know how to make bets doesn't necessarily mean we know how to avoid the pitfalls of Craps. Many casinos will slightly alter the rules of the game; you may be expecting one payoff, but get another, and by the time you discover this, you will have already lost unnecessarily. In addition, just because we know that some bets are called "good" by the general consensus of gaming authors and experts, while others are called "bad," this doesn't mean that they are either good or bad to bet. What all this actually means is that, by mathematical analysis, the general expected percentages are as shown, and, therefore, the house edge on such bets is as shown.

While Craps is mostly about the numbers—much more so than perhaps any other casino table game—reliance on merely these mathematical models is not the road to financial success at playing Craps. To make truly powerful profits from Craps you must not confine yourself to making merely the statistically "good" bets. As any successful businessman will tell you, taking risks is a prerequisite to success. Facing such huge risks, and their accompanying losses, but being able to navigate through these pitfalls and manage the outcome, is what separates the "wanna-bes" from the "haves." Those who "have," achieved their success not by being careful, but by being mindful, intuitive, observant, and able to act on opportunities that presented themselves at crucial times. Applied to Craps, this simply means that when opportunities present themselves [which, by their very nature indicate that their mathematical models would advise you to consider them as "bad bets"), that's the time to act on them, to make these bets even if they may be considered as "bad" or "ugly."

Craps is a game founded on the flawed principles of event-occurrence theory, usually called "probability calculus." Although useful as a tool to gain an understanding into the universal window of the frequencies of occurrence, this is merely an artificial construct made by man to facilitate a need for pattern recognition. Hence, all such percentages and mathematics applied to this game, or to any other, are merely concocted falsehoods, neatly tied by theoretical ribbons into a package wrapped in assumptions, but containing nothing.

It is perhaps an unfortunate reality, but a *reality* nonetheless, that the universe is composed of chaos, in which we, the pseudo-rationalistic humans, are hell-bent on trying to fathom a reason behind the chaos. There is none. All there is, is whatever happens to work at any given moment. This is what I call the "workability principle." Sadly, just about all our so-called "science" is still laboring under the misperception that there are "laws of nature" or "scientific truths." Although truisms may be used as examples of rationalist dogma, "truth" and "truisms" are nothing even akin to each other. Our ability to alter the universe to suit ourselves, such as making cities, cars, machines, and so on, is okay within the framework of the assumptive "science," whereby we have observed that on most occasions "if this, then that, therefore, this and that." This is often called "deductive reasoning in an inductive connective," a model for deriving absolutes from a set of assumptions faced with indefinable variables. It is, however, "workable" in most of the circumstances to which it is being applied and, therefore, we are able to have things like toasters, cars, TVs, and cable.

The fallacies of such thinking, however, stick out like sore thumbs in gambling games. Just because a game is called statistically a "negative expectation" game doesn't mean it won't pay. The purpose of gambling is not to exploit the inherent mathematics and percentages in the game, but to make money. To win. This does not mean that such can only be accomplished by reliance on the so-called "tried and true" models of probability, percentages, and house edge. These may be useful as "pointers" in determining your approach to the game, but to use them as a reliance, or as the founding principles of reliance strategy, is fundamentally flawed.

Success in Craps, and in gambling in general, is not measured by how close you came to realizing the game's inherent percentages, but by how much you won. In fact, by whether or not you won at all. It is the amount of money you either have, or don't have, at the end of your session, or playing time, or casino visit, that determines whether you succeed or fail. To hell with the statistics! If you don't have any money left when you leave the game, or the casino, what good is the fact that you achieved the optimum play of a house edge below one percent? Did that mathematical model do you any good? If you're happy with being broke, then throw this book away, go dig a hole in the freeway, stick your head in it, and pretend you will never be hit by the next truck that comes along.

Craps should be fun, as all games should be fun. Most important, Craps should be profitable. I am not interested in writing to readers who are convinced that losing is okay. Losing money may be a part of the gambling process, and will be inevitable, but it is *never* okay. We tolerate losing events because we know that they happen, but we don't have to convince ourselves that they mean we are already losers and that, therefore, we will lose playing Craps— or any other gambling game. If we do our job correctly, learn what we can, and then apply the "workability principle," we will know when to bet the least, or leave the game, to avoid exposure to negative events, while also knowing when to bet more—even bet the "bad" and "ugly" bets—because we are recognizing the opportunities that have presented themselves, in this time, in this slice of the universal reality, in these events, this moment, no matter how short. That's how we make powerful profits from Craps.

To be able to do this, and to understand it, we now delve deeper into the traditional analysis of what exactly is a "good," "bad," or "ugly" bet, and why. Keep in mind what I have just written—knowing this is important; playing, or avoiding playing, these events just because of this information is wrong. Your *skilled judgment* is the defining difference between the customary betting behavior derived purely from the statistical model and the inspired winning of *knowledgeable* winners. So learn, and *learn to adapt* what you have learned.

THE GOOD

Pass Line and Come

If you paid attention to Chapter One, then you know that the base bets on the pass line and the original base bet on the come both face a house edge of a mere 1.4 percent. This is "good," statistically speaking. Again, as with everything that follows in this chapter, please remember what I have said about statistics. Here, they become useful as a *guideline*, to describe what the traditional thinking indicates these bets to be, and why such thinking describes them as belonging to one of the three categories: good, bad, or ugly.

The reason why these two bets are considered "good" is that the low house edge indicates fewer losses overall by players who consistently make these bets. Although these bets do not win or lose any more or less, comparatively speaking, than other bets on other casino games where the house edge, or implied odds, indicate similarities, the percentages indicated show that players will *lower* their expected losses on the pass line and come bets, relative to other available bets. This *lowering of losses* is important, because the fewer dollars you lose, the more you have with which to play, and the longer you will last at the game. It is for that simple reason that traditional thinking dictates such bets to be classified in the "good" category.

The overall house edge on these bets is derived from the fact that the house will pay you off at less than true odds. This is not necessarily a bad thing; we all know that the casinos must make money, because if they didn't there would not be any casinos and therefore we would not have anywhere to play—at least not the way we now understand casino gaming. These two bets, compared to other house edges in other casino games, are quite good. For example, a bet on the player hand in Baccarat will face about the same

1.4 percent house edge. A bet on the Banker hand will generally lower this house edge to about 1.1 percent, so this is marginally better than the base come and pass line bets in Craps. Some slot machines are set to hold only 2 percent for the casino, and so the difference in the Craps hold is better, even though the differences in overall fractions are virtually statistically insignificant. Nevertheless, the Craps player can, and does, enjoy some of the lowest house edges in all casino games. While Blackjack, when played with perfect strategy, can lower the house edge to almost zero, and playing Blackjack with card-counting or tiered wagering methods can actually yield a player-positive percentage expectation, Craps players can further erode the house edge on the pass line and come bets to virtual insignificance.

Every major casino offers Craps players the opportunity to back their pass line and come bets with free odds. These odds are paid at true odds, and therefore, the casino has no advantage over the player. It becomes an even proposition—either you win, or the casino wins, but there is no implied house edge on these free odds. Many casinos will offer players the possibility of making twice the pass line or come bet wagers as free odds. This is called "double odds." Simply put, this means to put twice the amount of your pass line or come bet behind the original wager, as a back-bet in free odds. So, if you have $10 on the pass line, you can make a $20 wager as a double-odds bet, either behind your pass line wager or behind your come bet. The pass line wagers you can back yourself, by placing your free odds bet directly behind your original pass line wager. To back up the come bet with free odds, you toss the amount of your odds bet to the dealer nearest you and call out something like, "Odds on my come." If you want to call the specific come number on which you happened to land, you can call this out as "Odds on my 9," in the event that you landed on the 9. This procedure can be repeated for each and every come bet you make. Since you can only make one optional pass line bet, you therefore can only make one pass line odds bet. However, you can make as many come bets as there are box numbers. Eventually, if you're lucky, you will have all the box numbers covered with your come bets, after which you should no longer make any more come bets because now each such bet would be either a press or an off-and-on. So, you press to increase the size of the wager, or you take your wins and ride the numbers as covered. Of course, you can also make place bets and buy bets on these same box numbers, but we will get to that a little later on.

By taking *single* odds, you are reducing the base house edge of 1.4 percent for the pass line and come bets, to about 0.85 percent. By taking *double* odds, which are the most frequently offered odds bet option in most major casinos, you are reducing the base house edge of 1.4 percent for the pass line and come bets to about 0.65 percent. A quite substantial statistical reduction, and that is another reason why the pass line and come bets are called "good." Now, your pass line and come bets become known as "pass line with odds," and "come with odds." It is important to understand the difference. A bet known only as "pass line," or as "come," means you are making the original, single wager, facing the house edge of 1.4 percent. After you take the odds, these bets now become known as the "odds bets," and therefore clearly shows that you are taking advantage of the house offer of free odds.

In some casinos, free odds are offered as 3x the bet, or as 5x, 10x, 25x, 50x, and even 100x odds. This simply means that you can make up to that times the amount of your original wager as your free odds bet. Since free odds pay at true odds, and you face no house edge, it is therefore very advantageous to you to take as many odds as you can. Taking full odds, for the maximum odds offered by that casino, while making the lowest possible pass line, or come, wa-

gers, is the best way to exploit the percentage differentials
in the lowering of implied house edges on these bets. By
taking 5x odds, you will lower the house edge on these bets
to about 0.32 percent. By taking 100x odds, you will lower
this to a mere 0.02 percent—just about nothing. This is
about as good as it gets in the game of Craps, statistically
speaking. Of course, this doesn't mean you are going to win
any money. All this means is that you are forcing the casino
to give you as good a bet as is possible, under the rules, conditions, and circumstances. Now, of course, you still have to
win the bet in order to make money. But, at least statistically, you are now getting essentially an even game, and for
that reason "pushing the house" on these bets can be to your
statistical advantage. Your monetary advantage—namely
your profits—will come from winning bets, which does not
necessarily mean winning *these* bets, or these bets *only,* as
we will see later. For now, realizing that the reason the pass
line and come bets are called "good" is because of these possibilities will enable you to gain the quickest, and easiest,
understanding of the traditional thinking approach to Craps.

The "dark side" is the opposite to the pass line and
come, and is called the "don't pass" and "don't come." These
bets face a house edge of a little less than 1.4 percent (1.397).
However, laying odds on these bets means that you will
have to wager more to win less. That's because, after the
come out roll, the "dark side" bettor becomes the statistical
favorite, because these bets win when a 7 is rolled, and the
7 can be rolled more ways than any other number. I'll talk
more about riding the dark side later. For now, just remember that the pass line and come bets are the simplest to
make, and offer the better odds bets, because you are betting
less to win more. That's the basic difference between the
"front line" and the "dark side." On the front line you wager
less to win more; on the dark side you have to wager more
to win less. Odds payoffs are slightly different as well.

Place the 6 and/or 8

Statistically speaking, this is another of the "good" bets in Craps. While the base bets on the pass line and come (and the dark side of these) face an average house edge of 1.4 percent, the place bets on the 6 and 8 face merely the small house edge of 1.5 percent. This is only about one tenth of a percentage point higher and, therefore, statistically insignificant. For all intents and purposes, the base bets on the pass line and come, and the place bets on the 6 and the 8, are the best bets on the front line for the right-way player among all the bets in Craps—with the exception of the free odds. The only reason why the 6 and 8 face any house edge at all is because the house shaves the true odds slightly in its favor, assuring itself of a steady win. But that is the normal procedure for all casino house–banked games, of which Craps is one. As casino players of these gambling games, we all know that, and consequently this should not be an issue that troubles us. All we are trying to do here is to find out which of the bets are better for us, because these are the ones where the house edge is lowest, overall. In the same way as the house tries to assure itself of steady profits by paying off bets at less than true odds, from which practice the house edge is thus derived, we as players also try to minimize our exposure to theoretical statistical losses by finding, and exploiting, those bets in Craps that hold the least of that house-derived edge.

The reason why the 6 and the 8 can offer such a low house edge is that they can be rolled only one way less frequently than the 7. A 7 can be rolled six ways, while the 6 and 8 can be rolled five ways each. This means that after the come out roll, the 7 is the favorite, which is also why the "dark side" players are favored at that time. But the 6 and the 8 are the second favorite, because they can be rolled five ways each. This is why the base place bets on the 6 and 8 face only such a relatively small house edge.

Although this is not necessarily the accepted way of looking at this, you can, if you wish, look at any place bets on the 6 and the 8 that are made *together* as a *group.* A playing strategy based on groups is particularly good in Roulette, but it can also be applied to Craps. In this case, you could choose to look at both place bets on the 6 and the 8 and a combined group wager. You then have ten ways to roll a winner, while only six ways to roll a loser (any 7, which will end the roll). The combined house edge on these two bets is, statistically, the same, because each bet still faces the same odds, and each is an independent event of which there can be only the one such event after any roll (only one of the group can ever be rolled at any one time). However, practically speaking under the workability principle, the fact cannot be denied that when both place bets on the 6 and the 8 are made together, and considered as a single wager, that there are five ways to roll the 6, and five ways to roll the 8, which equals ten ways to roll a winner.

This kind of thinking can be applied to all place bets, and in fact to all groups of bets. However, if we add, for example, place bets on the 5 and the 9, and now have a group of four bets as our "perceptual group wager," then the odds are different, because now we face a house edge of 4 percent on the 5 and the 9. As an exercise, we can determine the perceived combined house edge of these group wagers as follows: add the house edge for each wager, then divide by the number of wagers. In our example, as follows: 1.5 + 1.5 + 4 + 4 = 11, or a combined 11 percent house edge; however, that is still not correct. Divide that by the number of wagers, which is four (6, 8, 5, and 9 as our four place bets), and we get an average house edge of 2.75 percent for the combined wager.

This is an interesting way of looking at your bets. You still have to remember that each roll of the dice is an *independent* event. Therefore, each number placed faces its own house edge, which is constant. Just because we are choosing to group our wagers doesn't mean that we are somehow altering the mathematical facts, as understood under the definitions inherent in that science. Nevertheless, *perceptually,* we can actually determine what the overall expected house edge would be if we could count our four place bet group together. By doing this, what we are actually accomplishing is a method of making wagers, and understanding them under the definitions of the house edge. So, while we are increasing the house edge from the 1.5 percent on the 6 and 8, we are reducing the house edge on the 5 and 9, overall. The average then becomes the 2.75 percent house edge for the group.

What this illustrates is a practice called "the diminished risk capacity" formula. By spreading more of our wagers among the place bets, as in this example, we are increasing the risk—in this case financial exposure—by betting more money on more events. However, at the same time we are considering these as a group wager, and, consequently, assigning them the combined value of "1," as opposed to the actual value of "4" (treating them as one wager, as opposed to the actual four wagers). Through this exercise, we are diminishing the overall risk by combining the exposure of the financial stake from four events to one combined event, and so reducing the overall house edge, in this example, to the 2.75 percent group constant, rather than the 1.5 percent for the 6 and 8, and the 4 percent for the 5 and the 9. This concept can, actually, be extended over any number of wagers, and indeed applied to any game whose rules of play permit it. The more events we cover—such as the all-across, for example—we can, conceptually, permit a general reduction of the house statistical edge over all of the individual events.

This becomes a more profound method when considering some of the higher house edge bets.

It's an interesting exercise whose application, and benefits, lie in the manner in which we choose to wager. We cannot alter the expected universe among each of these individual wagers, because they remain constant under the rules of this game. Since no roll of the two dice is anything other than a single, independent event, no amount of "conceptualizing" will ever change that, unless we choose to change the very foundations of the empirical sciences upon which these rules and calculations are based. So, if we accept the norm of the mathematical status quo, everything in Craps is its own single event. But—and here is where we, as players, can make a significant impact in our profitability— this doesn't prevent us from breaking the standard by creating for ourselves a combined method of groups, whereby we accept the statistical model but adapt it to how we choose to consider our money in action. And that's how we can overcome even an overall negative-expectation game, because by so doing we are concentrating on the exploitation of the *financial gain,* rather than the statistical edge.

In Craps, the statistical edge is always with the house on all bets, other than free odds. Therefore, our task, as players, is to develop wagering methods that enable us to concentrate on the financial benefits made possible by a conceptual shift in derived perspective. The diminished risk capacity model is a good example to use as a means of attaining the desired objective of financial gain, in the event that we require a fixed model upon which to hang our hat. In the final analysis, what we gain from this is the realization that each of the house edge percentages for all these wagers are merely an inductive, and not a deductive, measure. The lower each of these individual events is in negative edge against us, the better, while the lower the combined group, the better as well. Either way, the ultimate outcome simply means that among the range of wagers in any such group, only one such event can win at any one time. Therefore, the trick to using the group-perception situation as a means of combined wagering and diminished risk capacity application is to make such groups among those events that do not lose when one of them wins.

Placing the 6 and the 8, either individually or, hopefully, as a group along with the pass line wager plus odds is one such group. Assuming that neither is the point, if the 6 or the 8 wins, the pass line wagers don't lose. Similarly, if the point is rolled, the pass line wagers win, and the place bets on 6 and 8 don't lose. Adding the 5 and the 9, and buying the 4 and the 10, to any such wagering method can be done and is, in combined events, one of the better overall general methods of making the most from a hot roll. If the point is either the 6 or the 8, then the outcome of our wagering in this case is still the same. Whatever the point is, if it is rolled before any 7, the pass line wins, and our remaining place and buy bets (place bets on either the 6 or the 8, whichever is not the point at this time) don't lose. Similarly, if the point is either the 6 or the 8, and the other place or buy bets are rolled, then this wins and the pass line bets don't lose. Basically, this model exploits the combined lowest house edge wagers in a group that allows for the best use of the diminished risk capacity measure. Among these wagers, the only other wager that is even better is the free odds.

Free Odds

Free odds carry no house edge at all. Therefore, this is the best wager possible in the game of Craps, based on the equivalency of events in the statistical models governing the rules of the game. Unfortunately, you cannot make this wager by itself. First you have to make another wager, or wagers, on events where the house does have a built-in edge: for example, the pass line and come. As we have seen, among the range of base bets possible in Craps, these two are the best, carrying the lowest house edge among such wagers. Making a pass line wager, we face the house edge of 1.4 percent; same for any come bet. After the point is established, the rules of the game then allow us to add another wager to this one (or these, if a come bet or more than one come bet are also made). This is called "taking the odds," and means you are wagering additional amounts to back your bets. This is what is called the free odds.

By taking advantage of free odds, which carry no house edge, you are now getting the best of all possible wagers in Craps. Free odds are paid by the house at true odds, and therefore you and the house have exactly equal chances of winning or losing the odds wager. The house doesn't factor any "extra" money into this wager for itself, as it does for all the other bets in Craps. So, this is the only bet in Craps where you get an even game between you and the house. However, not so fast. Remember that you had to make another wager first, before you ever got the chance to make that great no-edge bet. These wagers, the pass line and come (or their dark side equivalent) *do* carry a house edge. So, what the house is actually doing here is telling you that it will let you make a no-edge bet, but first you must make another wager that *does* carry a house edge. The immediate effect of this is to force you to make a good wager at even odds, but make it in a combined group with a house wager where the house will "edge" you even on the free odds by using the group model we discussed above. This is the house using the same model of diminishing risk capacity against you.

Knowing that they will pay free odds at true odds, the house wants to assure itself of some kind of a win anyway, and that's how they do it. They force the first wager to be made on events where they have a built-in edge. Never-theless, this is a two-edged sword. While the house forces you to make a bet that is not even odds, you are still getting a base wager where the house edge is relatively quite low—the 1.4 percent on the pass line and come (and, or course, the don't on both). Also, by allowing the free odds, even with the prerequisite of first making the pass line and/or come wagers, you will be able to lower this house edge. Since free odds are made at no edge for the house, the com-bined group wager of the base bet plus the free odds reduces the overall statistical exposure to such events and lowers the house's expected percentage "hold."

As shown earlier, backing the pass line or come wagers with merely single odds reduces the house edge below one percent from the original 1.4 percent. By using the most commonly available double odds, the house edge lowers still further to a mere 0.65 percent. In those cases where more free odds are available, the house edge ebbs even lower still, all the way to the tiny 0.02 percent for 100x odds games. Think about it: make a $5 front-line bet, and back it with $500 in free odds. That's about as close as you can ever get in the game of Craps to an even game with the house. In Blackjack, using what I called my MBS (see *Powerful Profits from Blackjack*), you can get the game to about 0.01 percent house edge. That's about the same as these wagers in Craps. However, while in Blackjack you can actually alter the neg-ative expectation of the game into a player-positive expecta-tion game by several percent, in Craps that's not possible. In Blackjack, each hand dealt is a *dependent* event, whereby your odds of winning or losing are *directly dependent* on which cards have been dealt out and which, therefore, re-main to be dealt. In Craps, each roll of the dice is an *inde-pendent* event; therefore, it is not possible to change the overall expected house withholding percentage any lower than that 0.02 percent on front line bets with 100x odds. So, in Craps, we are always facing a negative-expectation game, even when the house allows us to use the free odds with no house edge, but forces us only to make this wager by first making another wager that *does* carry a house edge. Even though this percentage is actually tiny in comparison to many other bets in Craps—and other games and bets among the other casino games—nevertheless the standard mathematical fact remains that Craps cannot be made into an even game between you and the house, nor can it be made into a player-positive expectation game by the use of playing strategies and skills, such as are possible in Blackjack.

Disappointed? Don't be. No matter what this seems to say, the fact still remains that among all the casino games offered in any modern twenty-first-century casino, Craps is among the few house-banked games where you can get a series of wagers whose house withholding percentage is that small. This, therefore, makes Craps one of the best games in the casino, other than live Poker, which is not a house-banked game. Only Blackjack and Baccarat enjoy similar, or slightly better, house edge percentages. Consequently, taking advantage of the free odds offered in the game of Craps is a prerequisite to making powerful profits from Craps. If you ever intend to make pass line and come wagers, and you do not take at least double free odds, then you are wasting an opportunity, and you will never make profits from the game, no matter how lucky you get.

Of course, there are other bets in Craps, and making an overall profit from the game doesn't necessarily mean that you have to limit yourself to just the statistically advisable low house edge wagers. But since we are merely discussing the good, bad, and ugly bets in this chapter, as defined by their inherent house edge percentages, we will leave that strategy discussion for a little later on in this book. For now, the above five bets—pass line, come, place the 6, place the 8, and the free odds—are statistically the best bets in Craps.

What follows now are what I call the "bad" bets, although some of them can easily qualify for a "medium good" category. I will explain as we go along.

THE BAD

Within the mathematical framework of the established principles of statistical discussions as they apply to Craps, anything over 1.55 percent house edge is no longer a "good" bet. Unfortunately, there are several bets in Craps that can be made to good advantage, while still possessing a house edge that excludes them from the "good" bets category but doesn't quite put them into the "bad." Placing the 5 and 9 are among these wagers, which are perhaps best described as "medium bad." Simply put, these bets are just "not too bad," while at the same time being "not that good." I find them to be kind of halfway—a sort of Craps purgatory. There are several such wagers, and I'll begin with the two that are perhaps closest to this Craps purgatory.

Placing the 5 and/or the 9

These two place bets face the house edge of 4 percent. I have already used these place bets in an earlier example, when attempting to demonstrate a shift in perspective when considering wagers as groups. The 5 and the 9 can be rolled four ways each. If you land on them as a come bet, then you have the opportunity to back them up with free odds. As a come bet, if you land on either the 5 or the 9, or both if you make more than one come bet and these numbers are so rolled to cause your come bets to be put on these numbers, the base wager only faces the 1.4 percent edge, in the same way as the pass line (or the don't, of course). By exploiting the free odds, you can reduce the edge further, even on these numbers, as indeed on all come numbers so rolled. In effect, any come number so rolled becomes *your* point (in addition to whatever point may have already been established for the front line). Come bets play the same as the front line bets. The good news is that if your come bets land on the 5 or the 9, you can treat them as front line bets and take odds. The bad news is that they have to be rolled again, before any 7, to win. That's why *placing* the numbers often can be seen by players as having an advantage over the come bets. Although placing the 5 or the 9 will now expose you to the 4 percent house edge, which is considerably higher than if you were to land on them through the come bet, these place bets win when rolled just once before any 7, while the come bets have to be rolled twice to accomplish the same thing. Since come bets, and place bets, can only be made after the point has been established, this means that both methods of wagering are exposed to the dangerous any 7, and will lose if that dreaded 7 is rolled before any of these numbers. To land on either the 5 or the 9 through the come bet additionally means that either of these numbers first has to be rolled before any 7 while you have the bet in the come bet area, and then this same number has to be rolled again before that 7. So, your number must be rolled at least twice before any 7 for you to win anything.

Placing the 5 or the 9, or any number, means that you are able to collect the win the very first time the number is rolled. So, while another player may have a come bet, and you have placed the 5 and/or the 9, and one of these numbers is rolled, the come bet player will only now get to land on that number, while you are already collecting the win. By placing the 5 and/or the 9, you are facing a higher house edge, but get the chance to win even if the number is rolled only once. When landing on these numbers through the come, you are facing a lower house edge and have the opportunity to back your bet with free odds, but you must risk having that number rolled twice before you can collect. That's why placing the numbers is a good idea when using the 6 and the 8 as the place bets, and then combining two additional come bets with these two place bets and the pass line bet. This way, you are getting the best of the wagers, while facing the least possible combined house edge. More on strategies later on.

Placing the 5 and/or the 9 is a marginal decision. While placing the 6 and the 8 falls neatly into the "good" category, the 4 percent house edge on the 5 and the 9 make it difficult to recommend placing them, as opposed to landing on them through the come, having first placed the 6 and/or the 8. The only small advantage you may have to placing the 5 and the 9 is that you can take these bets "down" at any time. While come bets cannot be taken down, in the same manner as the original front line (and back line) bets cannot be taken down, any place bet can be removed from action by you, at no further risk or cost to you. A come bet can have the odds removed, by calling out, "Down on my odds," or, "Off with my odds," which then removes your odds from action; after the point or seven out they can be returned to you. However, the original come bet wager cannot be so removed, or called off or down. That's where the risk lies, as equally so the benefit of being able to back such bets with no-edge odds. When placing the 5 and the 9, you are more in control. You can see how the shooter is doing, and then decide what you want to do. If you place the 5 and/or the 9, and you hit one or both, you can then take the original bets down and keep them, as well as your profit, without further risk. This isn't possible with the original come bet, no matter on what number it lands. That bet stays until either won or lost.

This is one of the major reasons why place bets on the 5 and the 9 are better when made directly after the point has been established, or at any time after that but before any 7 is rolled. You can place these bets at the relatively medium house edge, don't have to wait for either number to be rolled twice before collecting a win, and are able to take the bets down at any time. For these reasons, placing the 5 and the 9 is a "medium bad" bet, "bad" only in the sense that it has more than 1.55 percent house edge, but not *too* bad because the house edge is still only 4 percent, and these bets can be manipulated by you through your skills in observation and anticipation. Generally, the best way to exploit the place bets and come bets would be to place the 6 and the 8 (or only one of these if the other is the point, of course), and then make the come bets. If the come bets land on the 5 or the 9, or both, so much the better. Nevertheless, there's still yet another approach to treating the 5 and the 9 as part of an overall strategy. You could place the 6 and the 8, and then place the 5 and the 9, and then buy the 4 and the 10 (leaving out of these whatever number happens to be the point, of course). We will talk more about buy bets a little further on, but if you want to place the 5 and the 9 to your best advantage, then use the four-group of place bets (5, 6, 8, and 9) and then the buy bets group of two (4 and 10). This way, you will be getting the best of these bets, at the highest win expectation, and with the combined lowest exposure to the house edge. It's, again, using the diminished risk capacity model, this time using the 5 and the 9 as your object of decision. As I've said, the 5 and the 9 are not that bad, and not that good. However, in combination with these other bets, using the place bet option and allowing for the place bet winners after only a onetime winning roll (as opposed to two on the come), with the option to take the bets down at any time, makes more sense; therefore, it allows the place bets on the 5 and the 9 to move closer to the "not too bad" category, the 4 percent house edge notwithstanding. That's about as good as these two place bets can be treated.

Placing or Buying the 4 and the 10

Placing the 4 and the 10 is most definitely among the "bad." Here, we are facing a house edge of almost 7 percent (6.67 percent, to be exact). This is getting into the category of "we just can't fix that anymore." Well, it could be looked at as "not too bad," but I don't like it, especially when you can get the same numbers as a buy bet, and only face a house edge of 4.8 percent. That's two whole percentage points *lower* than the same numbers as place bets. Why, then, would you *place* the 4 and the 10? Although buying the 4 and/or the 10 cannot truthfully be called "good," buying them instead of placing them becomes a lot better deal. Now, instead of a house edge close to 7 percent for the place bet, the buy bet lowers your statistical exposure to a mere 4.8 percent. This is just a tad higher than placing the 5 and the 9, and, as I have indicated above, even that can be called "not too bad."

While placing the 4 and the 10 is, to my mind, a "bad" bet, buying the 4 and the 10 is "almost good." This becomes even more profound if you can do what is often called "pushing the house." Such a practice applies to buy bets only, because buy bets pay off at true odds while the house charges a 5 percent commission (known as vigorish, or "vig," for short). Furthermore, if you were to *buy* the 5 and the 9, or the 6 and the 8, this also exposes you to a *higher* house edge than the place bet alternative—in addition to the vig. The house edge for the buy bet on the 6 and the 8 is 4.76 percent, while the house edge on the same numbers bet as *place* bets is only 1.5 percent each. The house edge on the 5 and the 9 as "buy" bets is also 4.76 percent, while as place bets they face a house edge of only 4 percent each. Buying the 4 and the 10, however, works in exactly the opposite way: it *lowers* the house edge versus their place bet alternative. That's why even these bets can be called "not too bad," although to my mind I cannot bring myself to put them in the "good" bet category listed above. The only way buying the 4 and the 10 could be elevated to the "almost good" category is in those cases where players can "push the house" into accepting a statistically stronger wager for the player—in effect, shaving the house edge down to a more player-friendly level. Here's how it can work:

The house charges a 5 percent vig for buy bets. Because on most tables casinos do not use chips in denominations lower than $1, when you buy the 4 and the 10 the house will charge you a minimum $1 vig (other than those very few and very rare casinos where you can still find "quarter craps," which is a game that uses 25-cent chips). So, if you were to buy the 4 or the 10, or both, for $10 each, you should be charged a 50-cent vig (5 percent of $10 = 50 cents). However, since most Craps tables do not use chips lower than $1, you will be charged that $1 even on these buy bets. This is silly, and has the effect of increasing the house edge on these bets substantially—and this, therefore, defeats the purpose of making these wagers. Consequently, you should never buy the 4 and the 10 for less than $20 each (5 percent of $20 = $1 vig). Now comes the interesting part. Same as when the house will charge you a $1 vig if you make a buy bet on the 4 and the 10 for less than $20, if you make a $25 buy bet on the 4 and the 10 the house will still only charge you that $1. Although, technically, you should be paying a $1.25 vig (5 percent of $25 = $1.25), the house will not mess with fractional chips, so you will still only be charged that $1 vig. This is what reduces the house edge to about 3.83 percent. So let's "push the house" a little more. What if you were to buy the 4 and the 10 for $30? Well, then you should be paying a $1.50 vig (5 percent of $30 = $1.50). But, well, the house can't use the 50-cent fraction, so you will be charged only the $1 vig (or should only be so charged—if the dealers want $2, call the Pit Boss and argue the point; most of the time you will win, and not have to pay more than a $1 vig even on this bet).

Let's go even further. What if you do this for $35? Now you should be paying a $1.75 vig (5 percent of $35 = $1.75). However, the same argument still applies—casinos don't use fractions. Now the dealers will usually ask you for a $2 vig, but you can argue the point. Mostly you will win the argument, and here's why: casinos are bound by gaming regulations *not* to overcharge! You can argue that asking you to pay them a $2 vig for a $1.75 true pay is overcharging, and, therefore, against the gaming regulations under which they hold their license. In most casinos you won't have to argue very much, and certainly not past this point if it goes this far. Casinos would rather have a happy customer than an angry customer who will leave the game and is likely to call their state's gaming control board to investigate their vig practices. It's a game, so to speak, with politics rather than dice.

But what if you could go even further, say $38 or $39? Well, at $38 you should be paying a $1.90 vig, and at $39 you should be paying a $1.95 vig. Now, we are really pushing the house. Here, at these levels, you might get a real argument from the dealer, the pit boss, and perhaps even the casino manager. However, it is still possible to be convincing and force them to agree using the above argument of "not overcharging" the customer. Your ultimate weapon in winning this argument is the regulation requiring casinos not to overcharge on vigs and wagers. Even that nickel could be counted as overcharging, and hence as a violation of gaming regulations.

Pushing this argument this far could really get ugly. You might be asked to leave the casino, and you might have to actually fight this under the regulations. You may not win the argument, because the margin of the $1 vig versus the $2 vig is so little at these bets. On the other hand, you might win the argument. There has been enough of a precedent made thus far, among casinos that do accept these wagers at the low vig of $1 even when you are supposed to pay $1.50, or $1.75, or $1.90, or $1.95, that you may win your case. Unfortunately, this may cause an ugly scene in the casino. Then, you may have to pursue the case in court. Somehow, it just doesn't seem worth it, although it is worth the effort to try. You can't lose by trying. If the casino will accept a $35 wager at the $1 vig, but not the $38 or the $39, then stay at the $35. You're still shaving the odds way down from what they were. Although still not a good wager overall, even with the approximate house edge of some 2.53 percent if you can get the casino to accept the $38 or $39 bet, it is still better than the standard 4.8 percent at the $20 bet level. Of course, you still need to actually *win* the bet to make the money, but doing all of this to lower the house edge can be accomplished and can be beneficial in those situations where you win by paying less for the better bet.

As you can hopefully see, placing the 4 and the 10 is never a good bet. Buying the 4 and the 10 for at least $25 is the best way to approach these numbers. Buying them for $35 is better still. Further pushing the house to accept the $38 or $39 wagers and still only pay $1 vig is better still. In the final tally, however, you still need the 4 and the 10 to be rolled before any 7. If not, well, then, all this has been much ado about nothing. But the next bet can be made in the same manner, and the next, and the next, and so on, since now you have pushed the house as far as they are willing to go. The next bet, or the next series of bets, may result in your positive win. You only need one hit on the buy 4 or 10 to make good money. Then you can take them down, at any time, as with the place bets. So, if you want to exploit the strategy of diminished risk capacity group wagers, bet the pass line with at least double odds, then place the 6 and the 8 for at least $6 each, preferably $12 to start; place the 5 and the 9 for at least $5 each; buy the 4 and the 10 for at least $25 each, preferably for $35; and pay only a $1 vig. Now you have all the best bets covered with the best chances of winning, the best odds, and the lowest house edge. That's about as good as it gets, by combining the "good" bets with the "almost good" bets, and these "bad" bets that are marginal enough to be forced into the "better of the bad bets" subcategory by the use of smart and knowledgeable wagering.

The Field

Okay, now we are getting to the "bad" side of the marginal, or medium, wagers in Craps. The field has a house edge of around 5.6 percent for games where *both* the 2 or the 12 pay 2:1, and a house edge of about 2.8 percent in games where either the 2 or the 12 pay 2:1 and the other number pays 3:1 (for example, a casino where any 2 bet on the field will pay 2:1 while any 12 on the field will pay 3:1; another casino may have this in reverse, where it will pay 2:1 for any 12 on the field, while paying 2:1 on any 2 on the field. Most casinos will play the field where both the 2 and the 12 will pay 2:1.).

The "field" is an area of the layout, quite prominent on the Craps table, showing the numbers: 2, 3, 4, 9, 10, 11, and 12. The numbers 2 and 12 are usually inside a marked spot, mostly circular in design, which indicate odds payoffs. While the remainder of the field numbers pay at 1:1, the 2 and the 12 usually pay off as 2:1. In some casinos, either the 2 or the 12 may pay off as 3:1 as a bonus (see Chapter One). There are 16 ways to win on a field number bet:

- One way   to make a 2
- Two ways   to make a 3

- Three ways   to make a 4
- Four ways   to make a 9
- Three ways   to make a 10
- Two ways   to make an 11
- One way   to make a 12

Add up the various ways to make the number, and you get 16 total ways to roll a winner for any field number wager. This looks like a great bet. So many ways to roll a winner, right? Well, not so fast. The field bet looks good, but in reality it isn't; it can't even be classified among the "good" bets, although it is marginal enough to maybe fall into the "not that good, but can be not too bad" slot. Here's why.

Consider the numbers that are *not* part of the field bet layout: 5, 6, 7, and 8. Curiously, but certainly not by chance, these are the four numbers that can be rolled in the most ways.

- Four ways   to roll a 5
- Five ways   to roll a 6
- Six ways   to roll a 7
- Five ways   to roll an 8

This makes a total of 20 ways to roll these numbers—add it up, it's right. Four ways + five ways + six ways + five ways = 20 ways to roll these numbers. So, while you can win a field bet in 16 ways, you can lose a field bet in 20 ways. This means there are 20 ways to roll a loser, and only 16 ways to roll a winner. Some simple math, and you find that the house edge is about 5.6 percent on tables where both the 2 and the 12 pay off at 2:1, and about 2.8 percent on those tables where either the 2 or the 12 pay off at 3:1.

Many players often think that because the field has so many numbers that betting the field regularly as part of a Craps playing strategy will result in overall profits. However, statistically speaking, as shown here, this is a fallacy. Anytime you have a wager where there are more ways to lose than there are ways to win, you have a bad bet. That's why the field cannot be classified among the "good" bets in Craps, even though there are some tables—such as those where the payoff is 3:1 on either the 2 or the 12—where the house edge falls sufficiently low for us to consider the field bets on those tables as among the "not too bad" Craps bets. Overall, however, the field is not nearly as good a bet as it appears to be.

Of course, this doesn't mean that the bet should never be made. Contrary to those writings by some Craps experts, the field can be an advantageous proposition, if used correctly as part of an overall spread. The same principles that make some of the worst bets in Roulette pay off can be applied to Craps. As previously indicated, through a group-bet strategy, Craps bets can be used to financial advantage, even though, perhaps, the statistical thinking may indicate that the individual bets in such groups aren't that great. As I have tried to show over and over again, reliance purely and only on the mathematical statistics and percentages to determine your bets will result in an overall loss. This is because even when making the most statistically advantageous bets in Craps, two facts will always remain. First, no matter how "good" the bets may be from that statistical perspective, this is still a negative expectation game. Therefore, no matter what, you will always lose in the end, if you only play this way. Second, you still have to win the bet. Even if you make only those statistically advantageous bets with the lowest house edge, you still have to win the bet. Both of these facts clearly show that relying purely and only on betting methods indicated by the mathematics of the game will inevitably lead you to a financial loss.

While most books will tell you that "if you want to win at Craps you can't make field bets," this kind of thinking is highly limiting, and exposes you to the inevitable doom of not just boredom with the game, but reliance on flawed statistical thinking as your guideline to success. It just won't work that way. For you to have financial success at Craps, you will have to make what would normally be called "risky" bets. No millionaire ever made his millions by betting his life's work and investments only on the "sure thing." For starters, there isn't any such thing. Everything is a "risk" of some sort. What there is is a difference between a "foolhardy" risk and a "calculated" risk. In life, as in Craps, using the diminished risk capacity model will allow you to take a calculated risk to your financial success, while recognizing that some part of that "risk portfolio" may have to be wagers that may be considered "statistically inappropriate."

I have myself a little chuckle when I read statements like "You can't win at Craps if you make field bets" or "Stay away from the proposition bets," and so on. While these bets may not be *statistically* appropriate, when we consider the game purely for analytical purposes, where else can you make the big money fast? Sure, you can bet big money on the pass line with 100x odds. However, no matter what the statistics indicate about the lowest possible house edge, what if you lose? Well, then you lost a whole lot of money really fast. What if you won exactly to the mathematical expectation? Well, then you wouldn't have "won" anything, because the math clearly shows that you will lose 0.02 percent of all such bets. Did this do you any good? Well, you can go home broke feeling proud of the fact that you lost exactly as little as the mathematics of the game indicated. But the operative word here is that you *lost!*

Making powerful profits from Craps is not simply an exercise in reliance on the statistical models, though they are useful as an explanation of the game and as a guideline. The larger issue here is, of course, to make money. To do so successfully, just as with any investment portfolio in any stock market, you have to balance your portfolio, and diversify. Some of your investments will be very conservative, and as much a "sure thing" as there can be in this world. Other parts of the portfolio may be considered "mildly aggressive," including those investments that carry a higher pay-off value but are not nearly as "safe" as the conservative portions of your portfolio. Finally, there will be those parts of your portfolio that will fall into the "aggressive" portion of your investments. These are the commitments usually known as "highly speculative," the ones that carry the highest risk, but also the greatest rewards. No self-respecting investment analyst would ever argue with an investment portfolio composed of these three elements, divided into financial portions that make sense for the individual investor.

Some people may wish to have 50 percent of this portfolio invested in the "highly speculative" portion, with the other 50 percent divided equally into the two remaining portions. Other people may wish to have 75 percent of their investments locked in the "very safe," and only the remaining 25 percent as speculative. It all depends on who you are, and what your money means to you at any given moment. It also relies heavily on what kind of money you want to make, and how fast. The more conservative your approach, the less you will make and the longer it will take. It will be more boring, but less risky. On the other hand, the aggressive player will risk more, but win more in much less time. In life, this is the same as in Craps. Those who invested in that little unknown Arizona company in 1983 were perhaps thought of as "highly aggressive" investors. Most people would have said that they were "statistically nuts" to put their money into something this speculative, this seemingly silly. For whatever it's worth, those who did so now have billions of dollars, and those who were mindful of the statistics and stayed away are now those looking for a retirement job because their 401(k)s have melted away. That small unknown company was, of course, Microsoft.

The point is, naturally, that the same approach must be utilized in Craps to make any kind of profits, especially because your exposure to the game will be so short and so finite. You don't have the time to play Craps over the millions of dice throws that went into the making of the statistics. You have 10 minutes at the table, or maybe an hour. Do you want this to be a grind for a dollar or two of "steady" risks? Or do you want this to be fun and very profitable? I choose the latter. I want the money, and fast. So, to do that, we have to diversify our investment portfolio. To do this, we must consider wagers such as the field. Otherwise, we will not be able to make our investment portfolio pay off in the manner in which it can, and should.

Doing this doesn't mean that we are betting foolishly. On the contrary—betting only in accordance with the statistics is the foolhardy approach. Not only will that result in making the game of Craps a boring grind, but it will assure you of eventual loss. It's just so, and no amount of your conservative wishing will change it. To make your profits come true, you have to be *calculatingly aggressive.* This means spreading your risk and maximizing your profit potential, while at the same time diminishing your exposure to prolonged, and pronounced, losses. The field bets are an integral part of the approach to achieve this goal. We will discuss this again in the Strategy chapter. For now, remember that no matter how "bad" something may be shown in this chapter, it is being shown from the statistical perspective, in order to demonstrate to you the guidelines, and the general traditional advice, designed to provide you with the knowledge necessary to empower your profitable decisions later on, as you master Craps in more detail.

Buy and Lay Bets

I have already mentioned some of these bets. To recap, here are all the *buy* bets again, with the house edge:

- Buy the 6 and/or the 8 faces the house edge of 4.8 percent
- Buy the 5 and/or the 9 faces the house edge of 4.8 percent
- Buy the 4 and/or the 10 faces the house edge of 4.8 percent

Buy bet house percentages are constant, due to the 5 percent commission. However, as we have seen earlier, buy bets can be "pushed" to lower the house edge to about 2.6 percent by making wagers that exploit the house fractions, allowing for higher buy bets while still only paying the minimum commission (vig).

Lay bets are the "dark side" direct opposite to buy bets. They face a lower house edge, because after the point has been established, there are more ways to roll the roll-ending 7 than there are any of the individual numbers. Therefore, if you lay any of the box numbers instead of placing or buying them, you are therefore wagering that they will *not* be rolled, and therefore this makes the lay bets a slight favorite over the place or buy bets, in some cases. Here are the lay bets, and the house edge they face:

- Lay the 6 and/or the 8 faces the house edge of 4.0 percent
- Lay the 5 and/or the 9 faces the house edge of 3.2 percent
- Lay the 4 and/or the 10 faces the house edge of 2.4 percent

None of these bets can be considered "good," under the formula of the statistical thinking we are using here to demonstrate the Craps bets and their derived house edge. Some bets—like the buy 4 and/or 10 for $35 at a $1 vig for a lowered house edge of about 2.8 percent, and the lay bet on the 5 and the 9 for a house edge of 3.2 percent, and the lay bet on the 4 and the 10 for a house edge of 2.4 percent—can be considered "not too bad," under the definitions and parameters we have been using in this chapter. Nevertheless, as I have stated earlier, anything with a house edge over 1.55 percent cannot be called a "good" bet; therefore, all of these wagers are in this subsection of "bad" bets, overall. We must not forget, however, that in Craps much is fluid in the way we perceive it. While statistically these are all "bad" bets, some among them are "almost good." It's that "gray" area where we simply cannot qualify these bets as "either-or," firmly in one or the other category. It just depends. On what? Well, a number of factors and variables in the game, strategy, your approach, wagering methods, and so on. Also on the game, the table, the casino, the house rules, odds payoffs, any bonuses offered, and so on. So the best I can say for these buy and lay bets is that some are bad and others are not quite so bad, but none of them are good.

THE UGLY

Ah, yes. There are "ugly" bets in Craps. Again, the only reason why we call them "ugly" is because statistically they are so lousy. Each of these bets faces a horrendous house edge as compared to other bets available in Craps, as well as in comparison to bets available on other casino games. These are usually the bets with the "fancy" names, the bets that make Craps seem exciting. Many times you will see players coming up to the table and yelling something like: "Nickel on the Yo, Quarter on the Horn High Low, Deuce on each of the Hardways, Ten each Uptown and Five-Deuce Big Red on the Hop!" Sounds exciting, right? You betcha! Someone coming to a table and talking like this will amaze some, or perhaps most, of the players. They will think that this is a player who knows the game. They will sometimes follow this player's bets, because he talks a good game. All the time the dealers will smile, the pit boss will chuckle, and the casinos will love this yahoo. Why? Well, he really said this:

"I want $5 on the 11, knowing that I am facing a house edge of 16.67 percent if you pay me at 15 for 1, or a house edge of 11.1 percent if you pay me off at 15 to 1, even though I realize the true odds are 17 to 1 and you are screwing me for the balance."

Then he added:

"I also want $25 on the Horn, which are the numbers 2, 3, 11, and 12, which is the same as C & E, facing the house edge of 12.5 percent if the payoffs are the 'to 1,' or the house edge of 16.67 percent if the payoffs are 'for 1,' knowing that you are exploiting my stupidity because the true odds are 20 to 4. I also want to add that extra $5 chip on the number 2 for the 'low' high, knowing that I am furthermore screwing myself on an additional 16.67 percent house edge on that bet alone, fully realizing that you are all thinking what a prize idiot I really am, which I really am."

The third request was really this:

"I also want $2 on each of the Hardways bets, knowing that I am facing a house edge of about 11.1 percent if you pay odds 'to 1,' or some 16.67 percent if you pay odds 'for 1' on the 4 and the 10, knowing that the true odds are 8 to 1. I also know I am facing the house edge of about 9.09 percent for the hard 6 and 8 if you pay off at odds 'to 1,' and about 18.6 percent if you pay off at odds 'for 1,' when you pay me 9 to 1 or 9 for 1 while the true odds are actually 10 to 1, all the while realizing that I am truly a really bad Craps player."

Next:

"I also want the numbers 8, 9, and 10 as place bets for $10 each, which I called Uptown. I realize that the 8 faces a house edge of 1.5 percent—the best bet I called so far—the 9 faces the house edge of 4 percent—another of the better bets I made—and the 10 faces the house edge of 6.67 percent, which I should have really made as a buy bet instead but I was trying to impress these people and didn't want to change my Uptown call."

Finally, he said:

"I also want the any-7, and furthermore, I want it as a one-roll bet on the hop in the combination of a 5 and a 2, knowing that the any-7 faces a house edge of 16.67 percent, while the 'on the hop' provision limits me to only the one roll facing the additional house edge of 11.1 percent if you pay off at odds 'to 1,' or the house edge of 16.67 percent if you pay odds 'for 1,' completely realizing that the true odds on the any-7 are 6 to 1 while you will only pay me at 4 to 1, or, worse, only 4 for 1, and that idiotic provision on my bet making this on the hop, meaning that although the true odds of this non-pair on the hop bet are at 17 to 1, you will only pay me at 15 to 1 or, worse, only at 15 for 1."

Actually, all of this player's bets really mean this:

"To all the players, dealers, pit employees, and casino owners within earshot of my bellow, I hereby declare myself to be a prize sucker, an idiot, a Craps player who knows nothing but wants to look like he is an impressive gambler who knows everything, while in reality I am a born loser and an obnoxious ass who just wants to sound important, as if I actually knew something, which I don't."

There you have it—this is the kind of player you will find frequently at just about any Craps game anywhere. These are the players who think that by yelling out these "cool sounding" names they will somehow improve their image as Craps player. To the uninitiated, these players may seem like they know something. To the Craps dealers and the casino employees, they are just loudmouthed fools. These players usually don't know much more than the novices at the Craps table. They have learned these words and bets from watching some other yahoo do it, and they think that they will be big men at their table by also doing it.

Casinos love these "cool sounding" names for these really bad bets. The really good bets all seem to have boring sounding names like pass line with odds, place the 6 and the 8, come bet with odds (or the dark side opposite of these). It's not nearly so exciting as when someone walks up to the table and starts to holler all those colorful names of bets, which sound so great. What they actually are are bright packages—inside of which is crap. And that's where "craps" got its name. Actually, the game is a version of an old game called Hazard, which later became known as "craps" because the French called the number 1 on each die "krabs"; the English-speaking players perverted this into "craps." Nevertheless, if we use the modern colloquialism of the "crap" inside a bright package, we can get the idea in a most descriptive and meaningful manner, while at the same time pointing out the general stupidity of players who try to impress others by using slang terms to make their bad bets. (As a side note, the reason we identify the word "crap" with human and animal solid waste is because of Sir Thomas Crapper, the English lord and inventor of the water closet, which we today call the toilet. He invented this contraption for use by Queen Victoria in the late 1880s; she was the first monarch—the first *person* in the world to use this device. Henceforth, when the device became commonly available, it became known as "the crapper," after both its inventor and the material deposited in it. Just thought you'd like to know.)

While you will quite likely encounter some player like the one described above—a person so interested in appearing clever that he can't see how truly silly he looks—what is far more important to learn from this is the statistical inevitability of prolonged losses vested in these truly ugly bets. In keeping with the previously established premise—

that of using these statistical percentages merely as indicators, and not as the holy grail answer to Craps success—these bets, mostly known as "proposition" wagers, are important to understand for what they are and not for how they can be colorfully called out to impress other players.

The prime reason why these bets are most definitely in the "ugly" category is that their house withholding percentages are so astronomically high that only two other casino games even come close. Live Keno holds anywhere from 18 percent up to 43 percent for the house, on many bets. Nickel and quarter traditional reel Slot Machines hold anywhere from 7 percent to 25 percent for the house. These are the two worst bets in the casino, as far as understanding them within the defined parameters of the statistical model is concerned. The ugly bets in Craps are a very close third to these two other uglies.

Hard 6 or 8

The hard 6 can only be rolled one way: 3+3. The hard 8 can only be rolled one way: 4+4. Betting either the hard 6 or the hard 8 means you are wagering that they will be rolled just this one precise way, before any 7 and before they are rolled "easy," meaning in combinations other than these pairs. The true odds are 10:1, but the house will mostly only pay you at 9:1, leaving a house edge of 9.09 percent. In those casinos where you are paid at 9-1, the house edge will be about 13.3 percent.

While this is, statistically, a really bad bet, it does have a place in an overall Craps strategy, when we consider making groups of wagers designed to accomplish financial profits. The same applies to the other hardway bets, as well as to many of the proposition bets. However, we will leave that for later discussion. For now, we are simply illustrating the kinds of bets where the house is gaining a huge edge over the players. Even a short exposure to these wagers, when made singularly and without any plan and strategy in place, will cause a loss. The costs of these wagers is simply too high to accommodate any kind of reason for making them as single bets, without a prior plan and strategy that accommodates their high house withholding percentage.

Hard 4 or 10

The house edge is 11.1 percent for the hard 4 or 10 if the payoff is 7:1, and a house edge of 16.67 percent if the payoff is 7-1. The true odds are 8:1. Similar comments to those in the above paragraph for the hard 6 and 8 also apply here, to these hardway bets.

These four hardway bets are among the only six possible paired combinations on the Craps table layout, the other two being the Aces (1+1), and Boxcars (6+6), both the "craps" numbers. These craps pairs are not considered as "hardway" bets because they have their own designation and cannot be rolled "easy." There are other ways to make these pair bets, and these are the "on the hop" wagers. For example, you can call out, "Hard 8 on the hop," which means you are wagering that the hardway pair of 4+4 will be the very next roll. It's silly to do this, because you are now not only facing the high house edge on the hardway proposition, but additionally are limiting yourself to just the one roll, facing an even bigger house edge. What if the next roll was a five? Well, now you lose your hardway 8 on the hop. But if you simply let the bet be on the hardway 8, then it would still be in action, because on that proposition that bet loses only if it is rolled easy, or a 7 is rolled before it is rolled the hard way. Similarly so for the other hardways, the hard 6, the hard 4, and the hard 10.

The Snake Eyes (Aces) and Boxcars are different. Since they can only be rolled one way, the 1+1 and the 6+6, they cannot be rolled "easy." That's why they can't be called "hardways," even though (technically) they are. These can also be called as "on the hop," but why? They are already a one-roll proposition. If you want to bet them, bet them just the way they are already. No need to try to sound impressive and call silly things like, "Boxcars on the hop." They already *are* on the hop, so to speak, because this is already a one-roll bet.

On the Hop

These are one-roll propositions, usually not marked on the table layout. These bets can be made for any one roll of the dice, and can be made on any called combination. The most common examples of these bets are a one-roll wager on "Five Deuce on the Hop," meaning that the player is betting that the next roll will be a 7, limiting himself to just that one roll and in that one combination of a 2 and a 5, rather than just wagering on the any 7, which would win if a 7 was rolled on the next roll, regardless of whether it was rolled as a 5 and a 2. The "any 7" wager is marked on the table lay-out, and pays 4:1, with the true odds being 6:1, for a house edge of 16.67 percent (if the house only pays 4-1, the house edge climbs to an astonishing 18.76 percent—ugh!).

The "on the hop" wager is not marked on the table lay-out, but can be called for any two-dice numbered combination, not only the number 7. You can call, for example, five-four on the hop. This is a wager on the number 9, to be rolled exactly as a 5 and a 4 on the very next roll. Such a non-pair on the hop-called bet faces a house edge of 11.1 percent if the house pays off at odds "to 1," or 16.67 percent if the house pays odds "for 1." The true odds are 17:1, but most casinos will only pay at either 15:1 or the lesser 15-1.

This wager can also be called a paired bet, such as "Little Joe on the Hop," meaning you wish to bet that the paired combination of 2+2 for the number 4 will be rolled exactly that way, as that precise pair, and exactly on the very next roll. You can do this for any possible pair, which are: 1+1 for the 2 (deuce, or snake eyes, also called post holes); 2+2 for the 4; 3+3 for the 6; 4+4 for the 8; 5+5 for the 10; and 6+6 for the 12. These are all the paired combinations possible in the game of Craps, using two six-sided dice.

The paired on the hop bets face a house edge of 13.89 percent for casinos that pay off at odds "to 1," and a house edge of 16.67 percent in those casinos where the pays are at "for 1." The true odds for such pairs on the hop are at 35:1, while most casinos will pay off at 30:1, or the lesser pay of 30-1.

Any 7

House edge of 16.67 percent (see above).

C&E (Any Craps and 11) and Horn

These are bets on the numbers 2, 3, 11, and 12, facing a house edge of 16.67 percent for craps and 11 (C&E), and 12.5 percent for the Horn. Horn high or low will face a house edge of 12.8 percent for those casinos paying odds at "to 1," and 16.67 percent for those casinos paying odds "for 1." The "Horn High Yo" faces a house edge of 12.2 percent in those casinos where the pays on odds are at "to 1," while all these propositions will face a steady house edge of 16.67 percent for any casino where the payoff on odds are at "for 1." Ugly!

Yo or Yo'leven

A bet on the number 11 as the next roll. Faces a house edge of 11.1 percent if the payoff is "to 1," and 16.67 percent if the house pays odds merely "for 1." True odds are 17:1, while casinos will only pay off either the 15:1 or the lesser 15-1.

Boxcars—the Number 12

Again, a one-roll proposition that the very next roll will be the paired combination of 6+6 for the total of 12. Faces a house edge of 13.9 percent in casinos paying odds at "to 1," or the ugly 16.67 percent in casinos paying the lesser "for 1." The true odds are 35:1, while the casinos will only pay off at either the 30:1 or the lesser 30-1.

Big 6 and Big 8—the Bonehead Bets

Finally, the ugliest of the uglies. I call this the "bonehead bet," because anyone making this either has a bone for a head, or a head without a brain, or no head at all. It's the dumbest bet in Craps, even a bigger prize sucker bet than the highest of the high-house-edge propositions. This is because this bet can be made as a place bet, which pays off with odds; making this bet as the Big 6 and/or the Big 8 means you are only getting even money—1:1. The very same bet made as a place bet on the 6 and/or the 8 will pay off at 7:6, facing the low house edge of only 1.5 percent, while the same wager on the Big 6 and/or Big 8 only pays off at even money and faces the huge house edge of 9.09 percent. Why in the world would anyone make this bet? Anyone who does will have "I am a prize sucker" firmly stamped upon his forehead. It is actually such a bad bet that several casinos have removed it from the table layout altogether. This only goes to show just how bad a bet this really is—if the casinos are ashamed of showing it, well, that's as bad as it gets. The casinos remove this bet from the layout because they know it's the ultimate of all Craps exploitation bets, and they don't want to be seen as screwing the customer. They are perfectly fine with keeping their other high-edge bets, such as the propositions, where they can hold anywhere from 9 percent to over 18 percent in some cases. Those bets are generally hidden and their large house edges not so prominently displayed. But the Big 6 and the Big 8 are just so pronounced, and so clearly seen, that some casinos don't want to be called on the carpet to try to explain why they are offering a lousy even-money bet when the same numbers can be placed with odds at several hundred percent lower house edge, comparatively speaking. This is particularly true for some of the newer gaming jurisdictions and some East Coast casinos, where the regulatory agencies have sharper eyes when it comes to holding casinos responsible for keeping their bets understandable for the majority of the simple gaming public.

Nevertheless, the Big 6 and the Big 8 are part of the traditional Craps table layout. Removing them should not be a regulatory requirement, nor should casinos feel ashamed of offering this bet. Just because this is such a dumb bet doesn't mean it shouldn't be offered. Why should the casino have to remove it? Isn't it up to the players to learn to avoid it? Well, yes. That's one of the reasons why this book is being written. I hope you will learn to avoid this lousy bet, and explain it to anyone you see making it. Unless, of course, you really don't like that person, in which case you can chuckle along with the dealers as this prize sucker loses his or her money on these idiotic bets.

And that, dear friends, is as ugly as Craps can get!

Keys to Winning

In each of my books in the *Powerful Profits* series, I include a chapter on the "Keys to Winning." These are principles of gambling, personal attitude, financial discipline, and other factors, which, when combined, directly influence your ability to make powerful profits from the game being discussed. Winning at gambling is not hard—*keeping* the money you won is *very* hard. Knowing how to win consistently, and then keep the profits, is even harder. There are no hard-and-fast answers to continued success when gambling. Each person is different, and therefore any advice that commands absolute adherence to whatever principles are being stated, is inherently flawed. I cannot anticipate what kind of a person you are, or what your personality, temperament, financial stability, emotional reliance, and personal abilities may be. Nor can I anticipate your financial situation or the reasons for your interest in gambling and gambling games. What I can offer are guidelines and principles of living within the lifestyle of the casino player. These are principles designed to show you the way, to assist you in your own determination of your own approach, skills, abilities, destiny, and financial results, or failure.

How you use these "keys" will decide which doors you will be able to unlock, and which you won't. To be successful, all these keys should be in your pocket, ready to be taken out at a moment's notice to unlock whichever door you are facing in that moment. I can't help you with how you use this information, but I can show you what this information means and how it can be best applied. You, then, have to take over, and further the cause of the successful journey not merely by learning this, but also by finding out how best to use it as it applies to your own particular situation. The same set of answers will not mean the same thing to different people, and neither will the same set of guidelines have exactly the same application to each and every person reading it. Here, we are discussing the game of Craps. This can be as exciting a game as you want it to be, or as boring and steady as you wish. It can be a very slow game, for steady profits, or it can be a very fast, heart-pounding game with big wins and big risks. Or it can be a game in the middle of this, a balance that can only be struck after you have mastered not just the game, and the knowledge of the game, but the other principles shown here in these Keys to Winning.

Craps can very easily be used as the microcosm of life. Here in this one game you have the good, the bad, and the very bad—indeed, the downright ugly, as we have seen in the previous chapter. This can also be applied to the people, as well as the game. Craps is a highly social game, and most definitely not for the fainthearted. A good Craps game will be crowded with many people, and there will be much shouting, and a lot of really odd behavior. It will easily become hard to keep your head straight, with all those noisy distractions, but that's precisely what you have to do—keep your head straight and your mind focused, and never deviate from whatever betting and gaming approach you have mastered for this game, or this session. We will discuss some strategies later, but the most important strategy is your own self-reliance, your own abilities, and above all, your ability to remain steady and focused. The distractions in the game of Craps are many, and they will be exhibited, and felt, far more profoundly in this game than any other gambling game available in the modern casino. Make no mistake about it, and harbor no illusions. You will be faced with the ugliest of players, and the most complex-appearing game. It's a quagmire of the slush of the world, upon which there are a few islands of peace and paradise. Stand on those, firmly planted in your knowledge of the game, your strategy, and these Keys to Winning.

In most books on Craps, authors have singled out several principles for steady success for beating the game. Among these, the following have found their way into the majority of the books and texts and are universally accepted by Craps experts as tried-and-true principles upon which to base your success as a Craps player.

1. Knowledge of the game
2. Sufficient bankroll
3. Money management
4. Discipline

By all means, these are several of the key ingredients that any player of Craps should acquire in order to assure, at the very least, a reasonable success in the game. Unfortunately, there are some major problems with one of these suggestions—Item number 3.

The major problem I see with the above time-honored principles of Craps success is overreliance on what has vacuously been called "money management." Well, what exactly is this? Many people have written about money manage-

ment. Some hold this to be the "holy grail" of Craps success. It's basically a whole bunch of hot air. Money management is nothing more than some common sense along with
a dash of self-discipline. In a nutshell, this means "Don't
blow your whole wad when you first walk into the casino."
It can also mean "Don't give back your winnings." Because
of this admonishment, many Craps writers will expand and
exalt money management as some kind of a heroic quest. It
just means that you should try to hold on to your money
and make it last for your entire visit, instead of dumping it
all at once.

Other writers also seem to suggest that you should treat
Craps as a job. As work, a daily grind, squeezing out the little percentages, the little tenths of a percent and even a hun-
dredth of a percent in lowered house edge—for the "long
haul." That's another favorite expression. Even I have used
it. It's a good way to indicate that the small bits add up over
time. However, these proponents of money management all
mostly seem to teach that you should make Craps your job,
or at least treat it as a job when you go to the casino. Why?
Do you have 10 years of your life to dedicate to becoming a
professional Craps player? If you don't, why would you
want to treat Craps as a job? Why would you want to go to a
casino on your vacation, on your weekend trip, or a visit for
whatever reason, and then stand there hour after hour and
grind it out bit by bit and treat the game as your other job?
You already have a job, right? If you treated Craps in this way,
you would be going from one job to the other. That's no fun.

Most people who wish to play Craps just want to have
fun—and win money. Have fun doing it, have a good time,
and have a relaxing time. There's no reason why this cannot
be so. You can play Craps successfully, and you do not have
to treat it as work. Yes, of course I don't want to waste my
bankroll, and neither should you. Even I have written in
previous books about the importance of money manage-

ment. Well, I was also wrong. Whatever the words "money management" may mean to you, to me this is simply part of the section that I call "Discipline."

Playing Craps is not your job, not your business; it is your *entertainment*. Because this form of *entertainment* can be done for profit, some very simple principles of discipline should be employed by you. This does not mean you have to be a hawk and watch your pennies like some accountant whose life depends on not making a "money management" error.

Your success in Craps, and your profits from Craps, will not depend on how well you learn "money management" techniques, but simply on what you do with the money you bring with you, and the money you win. That's *discipline*. What discipline or money management will mean to you is entirely dependent on what the value of your money is to you at that moment. Money management is nothing more than an accounting version of self-discipline designed to keep you from squandering your winnings.

Instead, the help that is being offered to you should focus on how you can better avoid becoming a victim to the distractions in the casinos, and particularly those found in the game of Craps. That is what I have called the "Discipline" part of my recommended Keys to Winning. Here, then, are my five categories for winning and making profits playing Craps:

1. Knowledge of the game
2. Patience
3. Bankroll
4. Persistence
5. Discipline

What do these mean? How do you apply them? Well, like this.

KNOWLEDGE OF THE GAME

This means knowing the game of Craps. Knowing the rules, how the game is played, what the various rule changes may be from casino to casino and perhaps even from table to table. It also means knowing how to bet, when to bet, when to do what is required during the course of the game, and how to do it. All of this essential information can be found in this book. Learn it, practice it, and become familiar with it. This is the foundation stone of the house you will build, which will be called "Your House of Craps Profits."

Knowledge of the game also means never having to guess. All the strategies, rules, and actions that you will face in the game of casino Craps should be firmly planted in your memory. Your decisions should be automatic. There should never be a single moment when you don't know what to do. There should be no decisions for you to make, after you have decided on your wagers and wagering strategy.

After you first learn the rules of the game, which you cannot do without because otherwise you could not play, and after you learn the strategy portions of this book (in later chapters), from that point on you will be armed with the most powerful ammunition you can get in the game of Craps as it is now played in the casinos of the twenty-first century. With this armament, you will gain an edge over the game by employing the arsenal of tools that are being offered to you by the availability of the rules and options, which only you, as the player, can exploit. You will now be able to play Craps enjoyably, have fun, be relaxed, and have a great time. You will be able to take advantage of all the favorable bets that the casino will offer you, while never giving up anything or ever being caught at any disadvantage. You will simply and plainly have the best of all worlds. Your Craps playing experience will be rewarding, easy, and comfortable. What's most important, it will never be anything like a job.

PATIENCE

This means not getting frustrated when the dice seem to go against you. It also means not getting hotheaded when something that should work out doesn't. Patience means just that—to remain calm and in the game without altering your method of playing. Nothing will always be perfect, not in life and not in Craps. There will be times when you will lose. Be patient. It will turn around. Converse statistics are merely a trend to the negative extreme, and the opposite will also occur. Being patient in Craps simply means that you will not let your emotions destroy your capacity to keep playing your best game, and that you will also remind yourself that any streak against you will eventually be followed by a like extreme in your favor. Patience also means that *you will not allow others to influence you, and talk you into bad decisions.* Most of all, patience means that you will always remember that your knowledge of the game allows you to play the best that the game can be played.

How can you apply this? Many strategy experts indicate that you should walk away from any table where you lose three to four rolls in a row. They say that this is an indication of a "cold" table or dice, or streaky rolls for the dark side players. This is wrong! Not only is three or four of anything not nearly an indicative sample, but if you become good at Craps, you can easily move your bets to the dark side and ride the cold streak for financial gain! Furthermore, even in the most rudimentary statistics, samplings of events this few in number render any decisions based upon such meager results as statistically useless. If you did this, and left every Craps table where you lose three or four rolls in a row, you will be spending most of your vacation or casino visit jumping from game to game.

In all of your playing sessions, streaks of several in a row, either as winners or as losers, will occur about 20 percent of the time. What does this mean? Well, first it means that such losing streaks happen only about twice out of each ten times you start a session of Craps. Therefore, it is not a frequent enough occurrence to warrant you to jump up and leave each time it happens. Second, it means that a statistical anomaly has occurred, and that the converse will also happen eventually. Three or four losing events are, however, not enough of an indication that this is an extended trend that can result in financial damage to you. If such a situation does occur, and you don't feel comfortable betting the dark side, the best you can do is to wait out a few rolls. In Craps, you can just stand around as long as you want, usually, and no one will pay you any mind unless the table is busy and other players want to get in, in which case you may be asked to make room for an active player. Usually as long as you have chips in the rail, you can wait out as many rolls as you want, and no one will bother you.

Patience also means that you do not let these minor trends or setbacks alter your playing style or playing decisions. Often what may seem like a "cold" table will turn just as quickly into a very favorable game indeed. By remaining patient throughout these series of a few bad rolls, and betting the minimum, or just waiting it out, you can outlast these anomalies and often wind up with a very large win when the situation turns around. Patience, therefore, is able to be applied to a wide variety of your Craps decisions.

BANKROLL

This is one part where I agree with everything that has ever been written about Craps. If you want to play Craps in a casino, you must have money. Otherwise, you can't play. It doesn't matter if this money is in the form of cash, a marker, or casino credit. However you slice it, money talks, and in casino Craps you must have it in order to play. "Bankroll," however, is something a little different from just having money. "Bankroll" is the designation that is given to a specified amount of money that you have dedicated to your gambling. More specifically, as it applies to Craps, bankroll is the amount of money that you have strictly dedicated to playing casino Craps.

How much money should be in your dedicated Craps bankroll? Well, that depends. Usually, a good rule to follow is to have a bankroll of no less than a hundred times your minimum expected wager. Therefore, if you intend to play Craps at the $5 table, with minimum bets of $5 per base wager, such as a $5 basic front line, come, or place bet, you should have a minimum Craps playing bankroll of $500. This does not mean you have to buy in for $500 each time at every table. All this means is that you have selected a certain amount that you are willing to risk, namely the $5 per. Therefore, in the process of protecting yourself against the inevitable losing streaks, you have also thereby given yourself an adequate supply of money so that your skills and abilities in the game can yield the profits to which you are entitled.

Being undercapitalized is a prescription for total disaster. If you cannot bring a bankroll of at least a hundred times the minimum bet, then don't play. By playing without an adequate bankroll, you will become scared in situations where you should make certain decisions, such as when to: go for the press or the proposition; or increase your odds to

25x, 50x, or even 100x; or perhaps back off your bets; or maybe take the dark side and lay the odds instead. Scared money flies away quickly. This is a gambler's proverb—and it is very true indeed. If you cannot afford a decent bankroll, stay away from the Craps tables until you get the bankroll that you should have. Why a hundred times the minimum bet? Because that's the safest gauge by which to ride out the bad streaks and still come out ahead in the end. I would actually prefer to recommend two hundred times the minimum bet, but this might get a little out of line with what most people will bring to the game, or are willing to allocate to a Craps experience.

Whether or not the 100x bankroll will be sufficient for you is also largely dependent on several factors. First, your ability to play Craps well, in accordance with your knowledge of the game and your mastery of whatever strategy you may be using. Second, on your ability to overcome problems and distractions. Third, on what the value of your money means to you at that moment. If you are a millionaire, and $500 is barely lunch money, then this bankroll advice won't mean much to you. If you are wealthy, you will probably be betting at $5,000 per roll, or even $50,000, or more. Nevertheless, the same principle applies. Bring at least a hundred times the amount of your minimum bet. Otherwise, you will most likely lose all of it, will play badly as a result of losing it, and then go and get more—and lose that as well. If you are a millionaire and money doesn't mean anything to you, and you insist on playing badly, then mail me the money instead. I'll be sure to make better use of it than the casino to whom you will lose it. Ah, well, wishful thinking.

The point here is well made for all of us who wish to play Craps as well as it possibly can be played, and to make profits. To make truly powerful profits from Craps, you will require mastery of, and adherence to, all five of my Keys to

Winning. It doesn't matter how wealthy you are. All that matters in regard to the bankroll is that you bring enough along to allow yourself the best possible series of circumstances available that will provide for a more rewarding, and certainly more profitable, gaming experience. Whatever the level at which you are willing to gamble, be it $5, $10, $25, $50, $100, or more per roll as your minimum bet, unless you have the most reliably structured bankroll, you will not be able to play Craps with the ammunition you need to make all of your playing opportunities pay off. That's why a bankroll is so important. An adequate bankroll will allow you to play at your best.

PERSISTENCE

Persistence and patience make you a stronger, more relaxed, and more reliable player. What is persistence? As it applies to Craps, it simply means not to give up when the going gets tough. You must have the longevity necessary to be able to achieve the winning events. While many people will be frightened when the dice turn bad, you should not be. If you are rational about this, you recognize that losing is inevitable. You will recognize that the opposite will also happen. Putting all the keys to winning into your pocket of skills will enable you not to be frightened by the adverse situations you will encounter.

While other people will act scared, and perhaps leave, or start to play wildly, making all sorts of weird bets, you will have the knowledge and rationale that will enable you to make the proper decisions. Applying persistence to your repertoire of skills will allow you not to give up when situations are adverse. This does not mean that you should blindly throw good money after bad. If you follow all of the principles in this book, this should never be of concern to you. Persistence means that you will not give up on your skills, on your knowledge, or on your ability to play Craps confidently and with an adequate bankroll. Persistence means that you will be able to stick to your game plan and remain confident in the knowledge that you are doing everything you can to maximize the profit potential of the game. Not giving up—that's what the issue is here. Bad things will happen, inevitably. How you handle these situations is what is going to separate you from the losers.

DISCIPLINE

This is the hardest but most important aspect of your Craps play. As this applies to casino Craps, there are two main categories that have the greatest effect on your success: handling the money, and handling the distractions.

What to do with one's money is part of discipline, and, in particular, part of self-discipline. The single most important fact that is missing from many of the texts on Craps that describe the principles behind money management is the fact of *the value of your money to you at the moment.* This is all relative to each and every person, and the value will be different for each and every person. Perhaps you are an average casino visitor, one of the millions of people who earn an average annual income of $40,000, go to a casino destination an average of twice a year, and stay for the average three days and four nights each visit. I'm not suggesting that this is actually you. These are general statistics derived from millions of interviews with people who come to Las Vegas, and used here only for the sake of this example.

Such statistically "average" persons will gamble about six hours per day, of which about two hours will be spent on table games, with an average total gambling budget of around $1,600. At this level this person can gamble at best only at the $5 table. Unfortunately, this is not always so. Most of these people gamble at stakes far higher, completely oblivious to any notion of any kind of monetary discipline. The result is that most of them will access additional funds and will, in fact, spend about three times as much in the end as they had initially thought would be necessary for their bankroll. Simply put, what this shows is that these people should have brought their entire bankroll with them in the beginning. Instead of just the mere $500 or so as an average allocated to Craps, and then having to access about three times more for a total of $1,500–$1,600 as a playing bankroll, these players should have brought their $1,600 with them as their starting Craps bankroll in the first place. This would have provided them with a range of bets and odds from the $5 base all the way up to 100x odds, and still have money left in the bankroll kitty. This $1,600 Craps bankroll would have provided them with a safe haven, and would have assured that they would be able to play Craps with the best possible chance for success. Instead, these people went broke, and kept running to the ATM machines for more cash, to the credit card machines, cashing checks, or signing markers—and losing it all in the end. It is here where the value of your money to you in the moment comes into focus.

If you are not concerned about the loss of $1,600, or more, then what good is any kind of advice about money management? What good is any kind of knowledge to you, or any kind of advice whatsoever? I'd say little to none. If your goal is to go on your casino trip and blow your money recklessly, then that's what you want to do and no amount of writing about how to protect your money will mean anything to you. Any advice about self-discipline as it applies to the handling of your money will only be valuable to you when it reaches the point where you become scared of the accumulated loss that your lack of such discipline could in-

flict upon you. This is the point of fear (and fear of consequences). It is this fear-factor that spans all frontiers between the average and the wealthy. No matter what the
value of your money may be to you in the moment, when
you reach the point where the loss of it, or any substantial
part of it, will cause you to fear the consequences, then and
only then will advice on money discipline be of value to
you. Now, you will listen, and learn. I hope.

I call this "money discipline." This is part of the overall
ability to control yourself, which is usually described as
self-discipline. Money discipline means knowing the value
of the money, whatever amount it may be for you, before
going to the Craps game. It means knowing the consequences
of the catastrophic loss of more than the allocated funds, or
even the major portion of the allocated bankroll. It means
knowing the value of the money won, relative to the output
of work that was required to acquire it in the first place. If
you earn your money at the average rate of $20 per hour,
which comes to about $41,600 per year in total income, and
you play Craps at a level where your expected win is at $30
per hour, and you are *unhappy* with that "small" amount,
then you have a problem with money discipline. Likewise,
if you play badly and are undercapitalized, and you are willing to risk your money at the hourly *loss* of $100 or more
(which is very common among the vast majority of the average players), then you are crazy. Of course, if you are a very
wealthy player, simply increase these amounts to the levels
at which you play, and then this will make sense to you as
well.

The two major problems that virtually all casino players
experience in regard to handling their money are:

1. Not being satisfied with what they perceive as wins
   that are "too small."
2. Risking high hourly losses in "chasing the big win,"

while using an inadequate bankroll to warrant such expectations.

For most people, their casino experience will be liberating. Here is an environment where everything is possible, all sorts of challenges are being offered, and vast rewards can be achieved. Well, the bigger the reward, the bigger the risk, or the longer the odds against it. That's the part that most of these people fail to understand or, more accurately, choose to ignore. To win a million dollars on a slot machine means you will be investing large sums of your money for what often are extended playing periods with odds against you in the several hundred million to one. You stand a better chance, odds wise, of falling into a vat of whiskey in Utah. However, it does happen (the winning, not the falling into the whiskey in Utah), and that's the allure of small wagers with big win potential. The problem is that often such wagers are *cumulatively far from small*.

In table games, and in Craps in particular, if you want to win a million dollars you will have to wager very large sums of money for long periods of time and play very well. Plus, you must be able to practice all the skills that have been outlined in this book, as well as master the art of money discipline. Yes, I call it an "art." To be able to handle your gambling money in a way that will retain the reality of it for you is truly an art. How do you do this? Again, it depends on you and your individual personality. Some of you may want to stash away little bits and pieces of your wins along the way, and thus split your money into smaller stacks, with some of these stacks hidden away and never touched. This will always assure you of having some money left, even if you lose all the rest of it. It's a good and safe way to assure yourself that you will never go home absolutely broke, but it is very hard to do in the spirit of the game and in the casino environment. Others may wish to allocate only parts of their overall bankroll to their Craps sessions and play at levels lower than those at which their bankrolls would indicate they can play. Many players may want to limit their playing sessions to specific financial goals, both winning and losing. For example, at a $5 table you may wish to play only until you win $50, or lose no more than $25. Or, you may wish to play for an hourly win of $80, and a loss of no more than $40. When any of these levels are reached, you stop playing and leave. Then you can stash some of your winnings, start another session, and do this all over again. Any of these methods can be useful, and are all achievable in standard Craps. Which one is better for you will depend on what you wish to achieve.

If your primary goal is to be entertained in the casino, then your money discipline is relative only to limiting your exposure to large losses. If your goal is primarily to win money at the Craps tables, then your money discipline will take on added importance. You will find for yourself a method that will allow you to keep more of your bring-in money and keep most of your wins. The way you safeguard your bring-in bankroll is by learning the game and playing it perfectly in accordance with all the other keys to winning that I have shown you, and applying whatever strategy you have decided to use. The way you safeguard your wins is both by continuing to play the game perfectly, and by allocating only a portion of your accumulated wins to any further sessions. As you win, you can add a portion of your wins to your starting bankroll. This will increase that bankroll. As that bankroll increases, you can rise to higher levels. There you will be achieving higher wins. Following this practice, you will continually be increasing both the stash of money that you have won and the amount of your playing bankroll. If you ever have a losing session, then you can simply lower your win expectation and go back to the lower level of play. When you have recovered from that loss, you will again be able to rise to the higher levels—and so on. In this way you will always assure yourself that you can:

1. Protect your starting bankroll.
2. Protect your wins.
3. Accumulate your wins and starting bankroll so that you can reach higher levels of play and higher profits.

It becomes a self-propagating process, and it is all directly relative to your perception of the value of the money to you during the moment and, hence, your ability to master money discipline as part of your overall personal self-discipline as specifically applied to the casino environment.

This brings me to the second of the two major problems for most people, and that is handling the distractions. There are many. All sorts of things are happening around you in the casino, especially in Craps. Craps tables and games are notoriously boisterous, especially when the players are winning, or at least think they are. People yelling, walking, drinking, smoking, laughing; music blaring; dealers dealing; people talking; pit bosses and pit staff offering comps or offering to track your play; cocktail servers asking for drinks and bringing drinks; overhead PA announcements and promotional announcements; smells; colors; slot machine sounds of jackpots ringing and coins falling into trays; cold air—all sorts of things, and one or more of those loud yahoos yelling out all those real fancy-sounding Craps bets, which you by now know are nothing more than an exercise in losing.

All of these will have an impact on your ability to maintain self-discipline and to practice money discipline. Everything around you is designed to liberate you from your rational thinking and comfortably settle you into mindless, thoughtless wagering. Everything in the casino environment is designed to distract you, to keep your head and mind spinning with so much input and so much excitement that the adrenaline takes over and all reason goes out the window. It is at this point where you will lose all of your discipline and therefore immediately become one of the crowd. That's precisely what makes the casino so much fun, and that's also precisely what the casinos are designed to be and to do. You aren't supposed to be able to think. You're just supposed to spend money.

All of us are susceptible to this influence. None of us is perfect. We all succumb to this allure and wind up in a daze, doing things with our money that we would never even think of doing outside of the casino or in our regular daily lives. That's also what's so liberating about the casino environment and atmosphere, so much fun—but it can be deadly. These distractions can easily lead you down the path of financial destruction. If, that is, you let them. By practicing money discipline, you will never be in this position. No matter what the distractions may be, you will be able to enjoy them and to experience that liberating thrill and adrenaline rush, but you will do so with the foreknowledge that you are able to keep a hold on your money. How well you do at this only you can answer. You won't succeed all the time. Even the best of us will fall into this trap and lose our place at one time or another. The point of discipline, however, is to limit the times when we fall off the wagon, and to instill in ourselves the principles of "value": the value of the money, the value of the wins, the value of the lowered losses, the value of the experiences and entertainment gained—and the value of the entire trip, when we can go back home and still have our money with us. Or, at least, some of it. Perhaps most of it, all of it, or even more of it. That's what money discipline, and discipline in general, will do for us in gambling.

Playing Craps means that you are already playing one of the better casino games. Playing Craps with these keys to winning, as well as all of the other information learned here, will mean that you are *playing for profit,* and you *know* you will make such a profit eventually. Plus, you know that you are doing all that is possible to limit your losses. This means that you have the full intention of not losing it all: bankroll or wins.

Gambling is the only form of entertainment where you can pay for this entertainment and after being so thoroughly entertained still go home with the money you brought, and even with more money than you started with. No other form of entertainment will allow you to do this. Therefore, when you choose Craps as your gaming entertainment, you are choosing one of the best games you can for actual profits. Discipline, therefore, does not have to mean "limiting yourself to unappetizing and boring drudgery." Instead, it should mean "allowing yourself the freedom to win." That is all that can ever be hoped for in anything: in Craps or in life in general. Acquiring your money discipline (and Craps discipline) is not a limiting experience. These are not chains that bind you. Rather, they are the ammunition for your success, the bridges for you to cross the wide chasms of trouble, the boats that sail you over the oceans of fear, and the rivers that give life. Together, these "Keys to Winning" unlock the opportunities that are in you, the opportunity to take the best that you possess and turn it even further into your advantage.

Avoiding Pitfalls

This chapter is designed to make you aware of some of the not-so-nice situations that can arise in the game of Craps. Some of these "cautions" will have to do with other players' behavior. Others concern the "sneaky" ways in which casinos subtly extract extra value from your bets, often without players being aware of it, or not becoming aware of it until it's too late, or, which is even worse, either not caring or ignoring such practices. It is a short chapter, but important. As nice as we all would like to believe other people are, some aren't. While I also frequently compliment casinos on how they conduct themselves in most major gaming jurisdictions, there are some areas where their subtle—and sometimes not so subtle—methods of extracting a few extra tenths of a percent edge from the player are very close to shady practices.

In many games, this is largely hidden, but it goes on every day. At around 3:00 A.M., just shortly after the start of the graveyard shift, casinos often change the gaming chips inside their machines. This is not illegal; all the casino has

118

to do is make sure that they notify the gaming control board, and then correctly alter the machine's payoff schedule to accommodate that change. Sometimes, these changes are very subtle. They are hard to notice on reel slots and reel video slots, but can be more easily seen on multigame machines, and on video keno and video poker machines.

For example, one of the most frequent changes to a video poker machine's program is the pay schedule showing the full house and flush payoffs. These are indicators of the kind of programming chip that runs the game. By looking at the changes in these two indicators, you can spot which machine has been recently "chipped" (an expression for the changing of the program). I use this as an example because that's the most visible change any trained casino player can easily spot. Other such changes are not that easy to spot. For example, a payoff may be changed from a pay of 15 coins for a three of a kind to a 10-coin payoff. If you're not careful, you can miss this easily. On some bonus games, such as deuces wild, for example, the changes can be so subtle that only the most aware will find them, such as the changes in payoffs for the five of a kind and the wild royal. All of these are clear indicators that the programming chip inside the machine, which runs the game, has been changed to a program that holds more money for the house.

SHAVED ODDS

You may now ask, what has all this to do with Craps? Well, several things. These examples show you how easily a casino game can be changed from one that pays off at a very low house edge to one with a much bigger house edge. Although these were examples with machines, Craps tables are very easily altered in remarkably similar ways. The most vile of these alterations, and the sneakiest, is changing the layout to pay off *for* 1 instead of *to* 1. Many casinos have gone to that these days, and it is about as exploitative as it can get. These casinos are banking on the sad fact that most of today's Craps players don't know anything about the game, and that the older players are far too few in number now. New Craps players, who have never played games with the traditional payoffs, will never know the difference. The casinos won't tell them, and although authors such as myself write about this in as clear a manner as we can muster, many Craps players won't read our books. Consequently, they wind up playing Craps on tables, and in casinos, where their payoffs have been so altered that they are now facing a house edge of sometimes more than 18 percent, but generally around 16.67 percent, when the traditional house edge was only 9 percent to 11 percent. While these traditional payoffs are still terrible, even at odds "to 1," changing them to an even higher house edge is purely and simply exploiting the players—the novices as well as the knowledgeable.

In trying to be fair to the casinos, I always attempt to see their side of the story. Craps has faltered in popularity. While this was the overwhelming game of choice among casinos players for some 40 years after the end of WW II, those players are now mostly dead. New casino players are the kids who grew up with video arcade games and, more recently, those who have known personal computers and computer games from the time they first opened their eyes. These players want fast games with fast results—brainless games that simply produce an either-or result: the spin is over in less than five seconds, and the result is immediate—you either win, or you lose. Although Craps is a really fast game, which offers many more betting opportunities than even the most sophisticated bonus video slot machine, it requires *learning*. As with most casino table games, Craps requires some mental effort, instead of just the act of wagering and finding out whether you won or lost. No one taught these new players how to play, and when they do find their way to the Craps tables, many just learn by doing it, or—which is worse—by watching and listening to some of the "smart-ass yahoos" who make all those fanciful bets which sound so "cool."

Casinos know this, and they exploit the innocence, the stupidity, and the lack of knowledge of the general run-of-the-mill casino Craps player, most of whom are novices. Casino Craps attracts a mere one percent of the gambling public. While 95 percent of all casino visitors will play Slots, and 86 percent will play Blackjack, only one percent will play Craps. Yet, Craps is the most costly of all table games to the casino. It requires a large table, taking up a lot of valuable floor space, enough to be occupied by eight slot machines, each of which can easily produce $1,000–$2,000 per month (or more) in gross drop, and don't need any employees to run them. Craps requires four employees per table—two dealers, a stickman, and the boxman, in addition to all the other pit employees. It is a highly human game. Players making correct bets can get the game to almost an even proposition between themselves and the casino. This means the casino isn't holding a lot of money on bets made by these players. So, the casino has to win a lot of events to make the game pay for itself. No wonder they try to squeeze as much of an edge out of the game as possible. I don't blame them. I am simply pointing out that they are doing it in a far too sneaky manner.

The first pitfall for you to avoid is playing on Craps table where any of the payoffs are listed on the payout as paying "for 1." Only play on tables where all of the payoffs are listed as "to 1." This will assure you of at least the better of the two evils: the evil of high house edge on bets paid at far less than true odds, and the evil of being exploited for a higher edge by getting even less for your wins. The fastest way you can find out this information is simply to look at the table's center propositions. If you see, for example, that this casino lists the payoff on the 12 as 30 *for* 1, and the 11 as a payoff at 15 *for* 1, then you know this casino has changed the game to one where they get more of your money by adding a huge extra house edge to their odds payoffs. In this casino, these two bets will carry a house edge of almost 17 percent on the 12, and 16.67 percent on the 11, as opposed to the traditional 13.89 percent on the 12 and about 9 percent for the 11.

However, please be aware that almost all casinos will now list the hardways as pays "for 1," even though they are actually the better pays of 9:1 and 7:1. These casinos will list the Hardways as paying 10 *for* 1 for the hard 6 and 8, and 8 *for* 1 for the hard 4 and 10. These are still the traditional payoffs of 9 to 1 for the hard 6 and 8, and 7 to 1 for the 4 and 10. Beware, however, of casinos that list the Hardways as paying 9 *for* 1 for the 6 and 8 and 7 *for* 1 for the 4 and 10. These are not the good "to 1" odds (relatively speaking, of course).

Later, in the chapters on strategy, I will often advise you not to play tables where the payoffs are listed as "for 1." Be careful not to confuse this with tables where the hardways in fact *do* pay the traditional payoffs, but may be listed as the 10 for 1 and 8 for 1, as mentioned above. The propositions caution I mention in this chapter applies primarily to the bets listed just below the Hardways layout, which are snake eyes, boxcars, horn, Yo, and Any 7. These are usually marked with the heading "One-Roll Bets." To make this easier, here is a chart that shows the good tables vs. the bad tables:

Good Tables		Bad Tables	
Hard 4 and 10 pays	7:1[a]	pays	7 for 1
Hard 6 and 8 pays	9:1[b]	pays	9 for 1
Any 7 pays	4:1[c]	pays	4 for 1
Any Craps	7:1	pays	7 for 1
Yo pays	30:1	pays	30 for 1
Snake Eyes pays	30:1	pays	30 for 1
Boxcars pays	30:1	pays	30 for 1

a. On some tables, this will be shown as 8 for 1, but it is still the better table, because this is the same as 7:1.

b. On some tables, this will be shown as 10 for 1, but it is still the better table, because this is the same as 9:1.

c. Often this may be shown as 5 for 1, but this is still the better table, because it is the same as the 4:1 payoff.

Even though these are still far from "good" bets, statistically speaking, it is very important to understand the difference. Casinos do this because it is easily hidden, and they can get away with this kind of misdirection. This becomes even more tricky when you consider mixed tables, where some parts of the layout will show pays as "to 1," while other pays will be shown as pays "for 1." On these tables, make sure that the Hardways are shown either as 8 for 1 for the 4 and 10, which is the same as the more correct 7:1; and 10 for 1 for the 6 and 8, which is the same as the more correct 9:1. Also watch out for the One Roll propositions being shown as "for 1," because that's the indicator of the extra house edge on these ugly bets. In the following chart, I show you the best table for all these mixed bets in Mixed Table One, and the worst version in the Mixed Table Two:

Mixed *Table One*—Better *of the Bad Bets*

Hard 4 and 10 pays	8 for 1
Hard 6 and 8 pays	10 for 1
Any 7 pays	5 for 1
Any Craps	7 to 1
Yo pays	30 to 1
Snake Eyes pays	30 to 1
Boxcars pays	30 to 1

Mixed *Table Two*—Worst *of the Bad Bets*

Hard 4 and 10 pays	8 for 1
Hard 6 and 8 pays	10 for 1
Any 7 pays	5 for 1
Any Craps	7 for 1
Yo pays	30 for 1
Snake Eyes pays	30 for 1
Boxcars pays	30 for 1

As you can see in Table Two, the Hardways are still listed as "for 1," but they are left at the better odds (relatively speaking, of course). The rest of the table has been shaved in the casino's favor, however. There are many Craps tables where there are such mixed payoffs. Some tables may show the Hardways as pays "to 1," while showing the remainder of the propositions as pays "for 1." Be wary of mixed table payoffs. Try to find a casino where all the propositions are listed as paying "to 1," and you will avoid the pitfall of the unwary. If you can't find a table where the pays are listed as "to 1," then look for a table where the pays are mixed as shown in Mixed Table One, above. That will be the best game, all things being relative. Although these are still not the best odds, and not the best bets, at least you won't be exploited because you won't know how to read the table layout, and what it means. So, this is the second pitfall you should avoid.

CHEATS

As is the case for all casino games, there are always people who are trying to find a way to beat the game, either legally or illegally. In Blackjack, for example, many card counters were able to take advantage of those systems of play. Although now no longer possible under the majority of circumstances, counting cards in Blackjack can still yield an often workable plan of play under ideal conditions. Card counting is *not* illegal, although casinos don't like counters because of the mistaken belief that they will win too much. In Craps, a similar skill was often used by some players to great advantage. This is called "sliding," and the players using it were called "sliders." It was a practiced skill, whereby—before the roll—the slider would stack the dice in the combination he wished to roll, and then "throw" the dice in a way in which they didn't fly across the table and bounce around, as is the common means of rolling, but would instead slide down the table's felt covering, coming to rest at the other end of the table, just slightly nudging the far wall, thus satisfying the legal-roll requirements but never actually "rolling," coming to rest in precisely that preset combination. Even now you see many players still stacking the dice, but then throwing them in the air, bouncing them off the felt and the walls, causing random rolls. The process of "stacking" is a relic from those sliders, and some players are still using that practice—even though they mostly have no idea that they cannot achieve the result for which this stacking procedure was originally used. It's mostly cosmetic now, and actually looks silly, if you know what's going on.

Although sliding the dice is not illegal, similarly to card counters casinos didn't like these sliders, because they could actually control the dice. To combat this, most of the dividing lines between the various layouts on casino Craps tables' felt covers are slightly raised; only by a fraction of a sixteenth of an inch, but high enough to cause any toss to tip the dice over and thus cause a random roll, instead of the slider's measured and stacked roll. Nice trick, and a nice way of combating it. As a result, sliders are all but extinct in Craps, and anyone still trying to do it will not be able to succeed in the vast majority of major U.S. casinos.

Some players have an uncanny knack for being able to roll consistently. Although the dice are as well-balanced as a human-made machine can make them, to a tolerance of thousandths of an inch, there are still some players who are able to control the dice in remarkable ways. Frank Scoblete, my friend and fellow gaming author and magazine columnist, writes about "rhythmic rollers." These are people who are able to roll in a "rhythm," and cause rolls whereby the dice come to rest in remarkably consistent combinations.

Although some players are able to control the dice, or at least appear to be able to do so in the short-term slices of overall probabilities when players are actually rolling at the Craps game, the inevitable fact will always remain that the dice have no memory, and therefore each and every roll of the dice is a completely independent event. Under these conditions, there is very little possibility of players being able to consistently roll the dice to achieve specified combinations.

Unless, that is, they are cheating. The expression "loaded dice" comes directly from Craps games where illegal and altered dice were used. These dice looked like any other dice, but were weighted by the use of, usually, lead additives, which weighed certain sides of the dice so that no matter how they were rolled, they would always come to a stop with that heavy side down, thereby exposing the side that made the desired winning combination on the upside of the two dice. Traditionally, this was the number 7, when the shooters wished to "pass" on the come out roll, but these loaded dice could be made for any of the possible combinations.

Nothing like this is possible in the modern casino. No casino would risk its gaming license to introduce loaded dice into a game. Surveillance technology is also so advanced now that not even the quickest dice-artist could switch the dice and get away with it. So, when you are playing, or shooting, you will be doing so with as perfectly balanced dice as are humanly possible to manufacture, and playing under the most stringently policed circumstances that can be found in gambling anywhere. Of course, this doesn't mean that you won't be exposed to bad bets, bad odds, cheats, or thieves.

Bad bets are part of the game. Bad odds are also part of the game, but when casinos start to shave these odds further in their favor, by paying off as odds "for 1" instead of the traditional "to 1," then you are not getting a very good game at all. As I have said, stay away from those games. Cheats will be found, but they will also be found out. There's very, very little chance that you will ever find yourself in a Craps game with a cheat. Even if you do, the cheat will most likely try to cheat the casino, and not you. So, this leaves us with thieves. Unfortunately, these are many, particularly so in Craps games. Therefore, the third pitfall you should avoid is becoming a victim of a chip thief.

THE THIEF

A chip thief is a person who appears to be just another player at the game, often leaning over the rail and making small front-line bets. Often, these are women, wearing low-cut blouses and exposing their assets as they lean out across the table. Since Craps is a game played mostly by men, this often causes the male players to take a good, long look. That's the time when the chip thief strikes. The woman may be the chip thief herself, or she can be working with a male partner. Such chip thieves will usually plant themselves close to the winningest player on the table, or the one with the most money: mostly, the player who has the most chips in the rail, with the highest denominations exposed. During any distraction, such as rolls of the dice, or whatever else may be happening, the chip thief will casually slide a hand—whichever hand he or she is not using—and carefully pinch one or more chips from the stack of the player directly nearest him/her, in a manner unnoticed by the player or the casino staff. By leaning forward, and usually sliding the second hand under his body to reach across and under the body to the player's chip rack on the other side, the chip thief also hides this from the overhead surveillance cameras, making this act very hard to detect. Often such a chip thief can easily steal several thousand dollars in a day and go undetected for weeks, even months. It's hard to detect, and the casino has to have absolute proof that this is actually being done and that this person was actually stealing. This is hard to do, and even harder to prove, unless the chip thief is clearly caught on the camera, at which point expulsion from the casino and prosecution become easier. Make no mistake about it—a chip thief who is caught will do significant hard time, because that's a very serious crime.

Unfortunately, chip thieves are so hard to detect, and so hard to prosecute successfully, that the usual alternative used by the casinos for any such suspected chip thief is simply to ask that person not to come back to that casino, or not to play Craps in that casino. Regardless of whether they can prove the acts, by just asking this person to go or not play Craps at that casino, such a casino can prevent itself from becoming a prolonged victim to such a chip thief's activities, and thereby also prevent their customers from being victimized. The best way for you to protect yourself from this, however, is by your own actions, and by your own awareness and discipline.

Chips thieves thrive on active games with a lot of play-ers. They seek out games where crowds gather, usually be-cause it's a hot game in the middle of a hot roll. While this is good for you, the player, it is also good for the chip thief. Try to avoid games with more people crowded around than the table can accommodate. These are usually games where people are standing two or three deep, behind those at the rail, often passing money back and forth to make their bets. These may be hot rolls, but they are a haven for thieves, es-pecially when you don't have your own space at the rail. While such games may be hot and profitable, and could, under better circumstances, be a viable candidate for your play, if you aren't at the table when this starts, or can't get a safe space at the rail, keep out. You can always find another game somewhere, and even if this was a monster roll, well, maybe you wouldn't be the one to benefit. You could have made bets the roller isn't rolling, and you could have be-come victim to a chip thief.

In games such as this, the chip thief will force his or her way to the rail and find a space, crowding himself (or her-self) right next to the liveliest player, or the one with the most chips, preferably exposed and in haphazard arrange-ment. A messy player means the player is unlikely to know exactly the amount of money he has on the rail, and this therefore makes it very easy for the chip thief to steal sev-eral of those chips, while the player will never know it. These chip thieves will also often have something else with them, like a large purse or a fanny pack, or something into which the chip thief can sneak the stolen chips without anyone seeing. Of course, the thief cannot keep these stolen chips on the rail, because they would immediately be seen there. So, another way you can detect a potential chip thief is to see if, first, they crowd close to you, and second, if they are carrying any kind of baggage or large coats. If a player crowds you, and you have lots of chips on the rail, and that player is also holding something—a purse, fanny pack, a large coat, or anything with cavities or pockets—beware. This could be a chip thief.

How do you avoid a chip thief? Well, there are several ways. If you are playing and have lots of chips in the rail, and someone crowds in next to you with all that equipment and stuff, then simply ask them not to crowd you. If they refuse, ask the dealers to move them over and give you space. The last thing a chip thief wants is for someone to cause attention to be focused on them. As soon as you do this, if that person is a chip thief, they will immediately leave you alone and move on. Of course, this doesn't mean that every person who does this will be a chip thief. They could just be another player, oblivious to the fact that they are causing you to be crowded, and as soon as you point it out to them they start to feel sorry and leave, or give you the space you need. Be nice, but insist on your own space. If these other payers are not chip thieves, they won't mind, and will give you room. If they are a chip thief, then they won't want the attention, and will also leave you alone. Of course, if you really don't feel comfortable, and for whatever reason these people become too much for you, and the dealers won't cooperate, you can always call the Pit Boss for a ruling, or simply leave the game. There's always another table and game somewhere. The best defense you have is that *you can leave.*

If you don't want to leave, because you may be doing very well in this game, the best ways to protect yourself against a potential chip thief is, first, always to know how much money you have in the rail, and second, to keep all your higher-denomination chips on the inside, framed on either side by the $1 chips, which will always be in play on any Craps table, regardless of limits (because of commissions and fractional odds payoffs). Let's assume that you have several $100 black chips, some $25 green chips, some

$5 red chips, and several $1 white chips. These are the most common denominations and colors of chips found in major casinos. To keep them safe from a potential chip thief, make a roll of your chips in the rail, like a sausage. Keep all your $100 black chips in the middle of this rolled sausage, then put the green $25 chips on either side of the black chips, then the $5 red chips on either side of this, and, finally, all the $1 chips on the outside ends. This way, the chip thief will never be able to easily take the high denomination chips. A chip thief survives by stealing the largest denomination chips he or she can, and doing so in as easy a manner as possible. Any player who arranges their Craps chips in the order of that "sausage" indicates to any chip thief that he is not a suitable target. It is simply too difficult for the chip thief to take any of the worthwhile chips from players using this method of defense.

Finally, protect yourself by never having your chips scattered, either on the table in front of you, or especially on the rail. Always have your chips neatly stacked in the rail, in the manner described above, and whenever you are making bets always stack your bets neatly and in a distinctively neat manner. That way everyone will always know that these are *your* bets, and *your* chips, and you will therefore be doubly guarded against any potential loss from a chip thief. However, you also should be mindful of your free odds, particularly on the pass line.

Sometimes, even if you are well guarded in your approach to keeping track of your money, and stacking your rail as described, you may forget the free odds. A clever chip thief can easily reach down to the table during the course of the heated game and remove either one, or all, of your chips from your free odds bet. This is harder to do for the chip thief, because, usually, they can only remove half the free odds to leave the single odds riding, to prevent this from being immediately identified. Sometimes it's worth it, because if you are distracted, or have not been paying attention to your free odds bets, then the chip thief can remove your bet and leave the game before you ever discover that this happened. In such a case, you're stuck with the loss, and no amount of pleading will ever cause your free odds bet to be returned, or paid off in case of a win. That's the most difficult situation to defend against, but also the one which can be easily prevented. Simply place your wagers immediately in front of you, with the free odds neatly stacked behind your original wager, and keep your hands on either side of the wager (on top of the rail, of course, because you can't reach into the table during the roll), in a manner that easily demonstrates, through body language, that you know you have the free odds there and are aware of what is going on and are protecting them.

You can also use a slight device called "off center." This is the placement of the free odds by you on a slight angle, or slightly skewed, so that only you know it and can see it. If at any time the dice hit this, and the dealer rearranges it, no matter. Just reach down and stack the free odds the way you want it. This way you will immediately be able to see if anyone has tried to mess with your chips. Any potential chip thief trying to steal your free odds will be in trouble, because you will be able to spot any changes in the setup of your free odds stack. If you see anything changed, and the dice didn't hit it, the dealers didn't touch it, the stickman didn't brush it, and you didn't change it, then there is only one way in which that arrangement could have been compromised, and that was because a chip thief tried to steal some or all of your free odds. If that is the case, immediately count the free odds; if a chip or two are missing, stop the game, call the pit boss, tell him you think there is a chip thief in the game, and ask for an immediate review of the surveillance camera covering your station at the table over the last few minutes. If you're wrong, well, no harm done. If you're right, the casino, and the other players, will thank you, because you will have spotted the most disgusting of all casino thieves, the Craps chip thief.

Before ending this chapter, I should assure you that the prevalence of chip thieves in the casinos is not that frequent. Mostly, if they are there, they will be at the big games, where they can easily wait for several hours to steal just one chip. Why would a thief risk being caught in a game where they can steal maybe $100, when they can bide their time in a bigger game and steal just one $5,000 chip, which makes their nut for the whole month, or week, or whatever? Most of you will play in Craps games where you may have several hundred dollars on the rail, so just keep your eye out, know how much money you have, keep your chips stacked in the sausage-roll, and watch your free odds. You will be very safe. I have not taken time to describe how chip thieves work in order to to frighten you into thinking that this is a huge problem. It isn't, and especially not so in most of the regular Craps games in which you are likely to play. But it is part of your overall game familiarity, and therefore you should know that it does happen, and learn how to guard against it.

Guarding against a potential chip thief will allow you to practice your other skills as well, such as keeping track of your money, your bets, and your incremental wagers. All of this together forms not only your understanding of the game, but also your comfort level with it. The more you know, the better your game will be, as well as your discipline and general comfort and safety. That's why even an infrequent situation such as the potential for a chip thief is still important to understand, and appreciate. Don't let this keep you from the game. It's a very rare occurrence, and it would be a shame if you misunderstood the point of this chapter, and it caused you to become negatively influenced against playing Craps, or trying to learn the game and exploit it for the great fun and profit it can provide.

The Dark Side

In any book on Craps, something must be said about the dark side plays. This is the "don't pass," the "don't come," and the "no" on any lay number. Traditionally called the "wrong way" plays, it has also been called "backsiding," since the betting line for the "don't pass" is located immediately at the rear of the pass line area on the table layout. Before the advent of the *Star Wars* phenomenon in the late 1970s, just about everyone called these plays simply the "wrong way," or the "don't." Then, as Darth Vader invaded our collective consciousness, these plays became known as "the dark side"—or "may the force *not* be with you" (apologies to George Lucas, the creator of *Star Wars*).

Simply put, players making bets on the don't pass, the don't come, or against the numbers are betting that the shooter will roll *losing* rolls. The reason why I call this the "losing rolls" is because, traditionally, the front line players are those hoping to "win," while the dark side players are hoping to "lose." Of course, when the right way players lose, the wrong way player wins, and vice versa, so in reality no matter what the outcome of the roll, some players will win on it and others will lose. However, to simplify Craps, the easiest way to look at it is that the shooter will generally be a front line player, so all frontliners are betting that the rolls will "win," while the dark side players are betting that the rolls will "lose"—colloquially speaking, of course. As a result of looking at Craps in this way, it becomes easy to distinguish between the kinds of wagers that can be made. The choice of wagers then becomes a simple "either-or" situation, and that's why it is important to look at Craps this way. Your choices to make bets in Craps come down to two:

- One, you will make bets on the front, *with* the shooter, wishing that the dice *do* pass; or
- Two, you will make bets on the dark side, *against* the shooter, wishing that the dice *don't* pass.

As a direct result of thinking of Craps in this way, your wagering and playing decisions become much simpler. You no longer have to confuse yourself about which bets do what, how, and when, or if any of your bets are in conflict with the others. Simply choose on which side you wish to bet and make your wagers accordingly. The rest will take care of itself, and you will never be confused.

When you are betting the front line, you are *taking* odds by betting *less* to win *more*. When you are betting the dark side, you are *laying* the odds, and betting *more* to win *less*.

The dark side is the direct opposite of the front line. It is like the other side of the coin. Everything that loses for the frontliner wins for the darksider. Everything that loses for the darksider wins for the frontliner.

On the come out roll, the front liner is the favorite, because his pass line bet will win if a 7 or an 11 is rolled. The darksider loses the "don't pass" bet on any of these rolls. Since there are six ways to roll any 7, and two ways to roll any 11, the pass line bettor has the advantage on the come out roll, because eight of the possible 36 combinations win for him. The don't pass bettor wins if a 2, 3, or 12 is rolled. Since there are only two ways to roll a 3, and only one each to roll a 2 or a 12, the don't pass bettor only has a four in 36 chance of winning the base don't pass bet. This changes dramatically if none of these are rolled on the come out roll. If neither the 7, 11, 2, 3, nor 12 is rolled on the come out roll, this obviously means that either a 4, 5, 6, 8, 9, or 10 was rolled. These are the box numbers, and, consequently, one of them now becomes the point. It is now that the players take, or lay, their odds. The frontliner will take odds on the pass line bet. The darksider will lay the odds on the don't pass bet. If the shooter rolls that same point number again before rolling any 7, then the pass line bets win and the don't pass bets lose. The frontliner is paid off for his pass line bet and odds, while the darksider loses the don't pass bet and odds.

Nevertheless, the darksider is statistically a favorite to win *after* the point has been established. This is because the dark side works directly the opposite to the front line. While on the come out roll the frontliner was the favorite and the darksider the underdog, after the point has been established, the situation reverses itself. Now the darksider is the favorite and the frontliner the merely hopeful underdog. The reason is the same as we have just shown for the frontliner before the come out roll—except that now this works in reverse.

After the point has been established, any 7 will lose for the frontliner but win for the dark side. Since any 7 can be rolled in six ways, but any of the point numbers can be rolled fewer ways than that, this makes the darksider the favorite to win after the point has been established. Now the darksider has more chances to win, while the pass line frontliner has to hope that the shooter will roll that same point number again before any 7. If the point is 4 or 10, then the frontliner only has three out of 36 possibilities to win, while the darksider always has the same six out of 36 chances to win. If the point is 5 or 9, then the frontliner only has four out of 36 chances to win, while the darksider still has the same six out of 36 for the any 7. If the point is 6 or 8, the frontliner has five chances out of 36. This is the closest to the darksider, and that's why points of 6 or 8 are the only two front line points that have nearly the same chances of being rolled as any 7. This is also why the numbers 6 and 8 are favorites among place bets, and not so favorite among lay bets.

DON'T PASS

To bet the don't pass dark side, you put your bet in the betting area marked "don't pass" on the table layout. You win if the come out roll is 2, 3, or 12; lose if it is 7 or 11; and if none of these is rolled, then a point has been established and now you have to wait to see if any 7 is rolled before that point number is rolled again. You can lay odds on your don't pass bet, in the same manner as you can take odds on the front line bets. To lay the odds, you have to know how much. Since everything on the dark side works in reverse to the front line, laying odds means you will be betting more to win less. The odds are, again, directly the opposite of front line odds, as follows:

Point Number	Front Line Odds	Dark Side Odds
4 or 10	2:1	1:2
5 or 9	3:2	2:3
6 or 8	6:5	5:6

Remember that free odds are paid off at true odds, and therefore there is no casino edge on these odds bets. You do, however, have to make a higher odds wager to win a lesser payoff because your don't pass (or don't come) bet is the favorite to win, after a point has been established. For example, let's say the point is 10, and you have made a $5 don't pass wager. Now, after the 10 was rolled to make it the point, you want to lay odds. If you want to lay single odds, you now have to bet $10 to win $5. While on the pass line you would only have to take the $5 odds and get paid $10 (which is 2:1), on the dark side don't pass bet you have to lay the $10 to win the $5 (which is 1:2). More to win less, but that is so because this bet is now a statistical favorite to win.

On the pass line, the odds bet is positioned directly behind the line bet. On the don't pass line this isn't possible, so because it's a don't pass bet, the odds now have to be identified. This is usually done by what is called "bridging" the bet. Since you now have the $5 don't pass bet, and you are now laying the $10 odds to win the $5 single odds wager, the bet will be arranged with the $5 single odds bet positioned directly next to the $5 base don't pass bet and the $5 payoff "bridged" over both these bets. This clearly shows that you have made a $5 base don't pass bet, and then are laying odds at $10 to win $5. Although fairly difficult to describe in words, when you actually see this in chips it will make abundant sense. To visualize what this actually looks like, take three cookies and put two of them on your plate side by side; then put the third cookie over the two so that it straddles them, with half of the top cookie over the right and the other half over the left, with the dividing edge between the two bottom cookies directly underneath the top cookie. It's kind of a "bridge," and that's why laying odds is called "bridging" the bet.

While there is no house edge on the free odds that you

lay, there is a house edge on the original bet, just as there is on the front line. The don't pass bet (and the don't come bet) share the same original wager house edge of 1.4 percent. By laying single odds, you can reduce the house edge, as is also the case for the frontliners. The higher the amount of the free odds the house allows you to lay, the lower the house edge on these combined bets. Most casinos will allow you to lay double odds. Many will offer 3x odds or 5x odds, and even 10x odds are common. Of course, some casinos will allow you up to 100x odds. Here's how it affects the edge:

Don't pass base wager	=	house edge of 1.4 percent
Don't pass with single odds	=	house edge of 0.82 percent
Don't pass with double odds	=	house edge of 0.61 percent
Don't pass with 3x odds	=	house edge of 0.45 percent
Don't pass with 5x odds	=	house edge of 0.31 percent
Don't pass with 10x odds	=	house edge of 0.17 percent
Don't pass with 100x odds	=	house edge of 0.015 percent

This is fractionally different to the pass line, but is so close as to be statistically considered as virtually identical. These odds and house edge lists are the same also for the don't come bets. As you can see, your dark side bets are a little better than the front line wagers, statistically, and are a slight favorite especially after the come out roll. That's one of the reasons why many players prefer to play the dark side. Unfortunately, these players are usually making their dark side betting decisions for the wrong reasons. Just because, statistically, the dark side is a little better off than the front line, this doesn't mean that it actually "means" anything profound. The differences are so small that you would have to wager tens of thousands of dollars, even millions, and for long periods of time, for these small fractional statistical advantages to actually mean something to your financial success in Craps. That's the same problem faced by the front line players; however, while the front line player may have the statistical disadvantage, they do have a *financial* advantage because they get paid more for risking less, while the darksider has to risk more to win less.

All things considered, the statistical advantages for the darksiders are far outweighed by the financial benefits the frontliners can enjoy. It's just not worth playing the dark side simply and only because the mathematics indicate that these bets are a tiny bit more favorable. If you are going to play the don't pass and don't come, then your reasons should be other than merely the reliance on the statistical percentages. Moving your action to the dark side should be a temporary move, based on your observation of the trends of the game in progress. Some shooters just will not roll points. Some dice, tables, and even series of events will simply reward the darksiders, and destroy the frontliners. In Craps you can win on both the winning rolls and the losing rolls. You have the opportunity to switch from one to the other, based on your own abilities and, particularly, your skills in measuring the pace of the game. If you see that this game is a "cold" game, meaning frontliners are frowning, then it's to your financial advantage to make the "don't" bets. We'll get into strategy decisions a little later, but for now just remember that making dark side your preferred method of wagering should be a decision based on your real-world play—particularly, on observation of the trends of the immediate game in progress—and not vested merely in the theoretical indicators that the wrong way is the better bet.

DON'T COME

"Don't come" is the same as don't pass, and is the direct opposite to the "come" bets. To make a don't come bet, you place your wager in the area on the table layout marked "don't come bar-12." This means that you are wagering that either the next roll will be 2 or 3; or, if the roll is any box number, that you wish for a 7 to be rolled before that box number is rolled again. The "bar-12" means that your don't come wager is "barred" from action if a 12 is rolled, and this is what provides the house part of its edge on these bets. (Barring the 12 is also done to prevent players from "middling" the bets, such as by making the front line and back line wagers at the same time; this way they would win on either 7, 11, 2, 3, or 12, covering their bets, and would now have a statistical advantage over the house because they would win on the pass and the point, as well as the crap-out. By barring the 12, the house, therefore, assures itself of an edge over even these players, and this consequently combines to provide a part of the overall house edge on these bets.)

If a 12 is rolled, your don't come bet is simply placed in limbo, a no-decision. It stays in action for the next roll, unless you pick it up, which you can do if you want. This bet will lose, however, if a 7 or an 11 is rolled immediately after you make the don't come bet. If the shooter rolls any number other than a 2, 3, 12, 11 or 7 on the roll immediately after you have made the don't come bet, the dealer will now place your wager behind the number that was rolled. For example, if the next roll after you made your don't come bet is, say, the 9, then the dealer will put your bet behind the number 9, in a small area immediately behind the number's layout, marked by a rectangle. This indicates to everyone that you have made a don't come bet, that the number rolled for your don't come was the 9, and that now your bet rides on the outcome of further rolls. If the 7 is rolled before the 9 is rolled again, you win. If the 9 is rolled before any 7, you lose. And so on for all the don't come bets, no matter on what numbers they may so land.

You can also back your don't come bet by laying the appropriate odds. Same as for the don't pass, the don't come odds bets work the same way, and pay off at the same odds as previously shown for the darksider. Again, as with the don't pass, you *lay* the odds. This you do by tossing the appropriate amount of money to the dealer and saying something like, "Lay odds on my don't come 9." These odds will be arranged by the dealer in a bridge, same as those for the don't pass, to indicate you are laying odds (again, more to win less, just like the don't pass). This can be repeated for as many times as there are don't come numbers available. If you keep making don't come bets, eventually you will have all the don't come numbers covered, at which stage it become moot to try and make others. Since any 7 has to be rolled before any of the don't come numbers can win, the more don't come numbers you have covered, the more times you will lose, because each time any of those numbers is rolled before any 7 that number loses. While the front line come bets can be made repeatedly, even if all numbers are covered—since then the bets will simply be off and on, or perhaps pressed—the don't come is useful only for one number, possibly two, and no more. The more don't come bets you have in action, the more you stand to lose if these numbers are rolled at any time before any 7. Betting the don't come is, therefore, not nearly as good as betting the front line come.

Most of the time, you will be better served if your don't come lands on the 4 or the 10. These are the only two numbers that may be a viable candidate for more than one don't come wager. In any case, to my mind, the don't come is a silly wager, with more ways to lose, cumulative with other such bets, than to win. If you want to bet against the numbers, then your better alternative is to lay the bets directly, instead of going through the don't come.

LAY BETS

A lay bet is actually supposed to be called the "don't come buy bet," while the right way buy bets are supposed to be called "do come buy bets." It's actually the same thing, but it makes it a little more clear. The lay bet is the direct opposite to the buy bet. That's why it is often better to refer to these bets as the "don't come buy bets," because the word "don't" easily and immediately shows that this is the dark side bet, the direct opposite of the frontliner's buy bet. No matter how this may be written in whatever book or text you may be reading, just remember that anytime anything is stated as a "don't," it is immediately identified in the game of Craps as a bet that is directly opposite to its more demonstrable front line cousin.

While a buy bet is made with the intention that the number so bet will be rolled before any 7, the lay bet (the "don't come buy bet') is made for exactly the opposite reason. A lay bet is made *against* the number, meaning that the bettor is risking his money because he thinks that the number so played will *not* be rolled before any 7. Often these bets are made by simply calling out something like "No 5," which immediately tells the dealer that you wish to make a lay bet against the number 5. The dealer will then put your lay bet behind that number and cap it with a marker indicating it to be a bet against that number. This bet will win if any 7 is rolled before that number—in our example the number 5—but lose if the 5 is rolled before any 7. Since there are six ways to roll any 7, and only four ways to roll a 5, this bet is statistically a favorite to win.

A lay bet can be made against any of the box numbers. The casino's edge against a lay bet is as follows:

Lay the 6 and 8	=	house edge of 4.1 percent
Lay the 5 and 9	=	house edge of 3.2 percent
Lay the 4 and 10	=	house edge of 2.4 percent

When making a lay bet, you must pay the house a commission, just as with the buy bet. However, unlike with buy bets, where you must make the commission payment based upon the amount of your wager, with lay bets you pay commission based on the expected payout. For example, if you lay $40 against the 10, your expected win is $20 (remember, payoffs are in reverse, so here 1:2), and therefore your 5 percent commission is $1. If you want to so bet against the 10, you would toss $41 to the dealer and say something like, "Lay the 10 for forty." Or, you could simply say, "$40 no 10." Either way, it's clear you are betting the $40 to win $20, and you are paying the house its 5 percent commission, which is $1 on the $20 possible win. And so on, for all the numbers, and their respective odds.

Of course, you can also try to push the house into accepting the $1 commission by making higher lay bets on the 4 and the 10, similarly to what we have already discussed with the situation of buying the 4 and the 10. It's the same thing, again, but in reverse. It's a little more tricky here, but you could, for example, try to lay $70 to win $35, which should be a $1.75 commission (5 percent of the $35 expected win at odds 1:2 = $1.75), and then still only ask to pay the $1 commission. If you can get away with it, then the lay bets against the 4 and the 10 will be a lot more advantageous to you than their buy bet front line alternatives. The simple reason is that if you lay the 4 and the 10, as here suggested, and shave the house on its commission, you will be getting a reasonably good bet because now the house edge on these bets will be below 2.1 percent. Furthermore, there are some casinos where you will be charged the commission *only after you win,* and *not* up front. You have to ask about this, but it's definitely worth your while. If you can get the house to accept the commission only after you win, then the house edge will become merely about 0.84 percent, and this will, therefore, make these lay bets among the best bets in the game, and will firmly plant them among the "good" bets, discussed earlier. The only reason I have not included these bets in the "good" category is because there are too many variables involved. First, you must be able to push the house into accepting the lower commission on such bets. Second, you must be able to find a Craps game where the house will accept the lay commissions only after the win. You might actually have to talk the house into accepting both these wagers, but if you do, you will be getting statistically the best possible chances for a win, facing what is essentially among the lowest house edge bets anywhere in the casino.

In the final analysis, it's all relative. Being a don't player has its advantages and its disadvantages. To my mind, the disadvantages far outweigh the advantages, except perhaps for the lay bets against the 4 and the 10 in a casino where you can push the house to accept the higher lay bets, and then also get them to accept the commission only after a win. Only on these two lay bets, and only in casinos where you can so get away with this, would I ever consider the dark side as a betting option. In most circumstances, the front line will be far more profitable, over short-term as well as long-term strategy play, than the dark side can ever be. Even though the dark side may have the statistical advantage in some circumstances, and can actually be a very good bet, such as the lay 4 and 10 we discussed here, still the overall facts remain that financial profits don't come easily when you have to risk more to win less. And that's why I don't like the dark side.

7

Winning Strategies
for Craps

If you're familiar with the TV game show *Family Feud,* you know that the key part of that show is when the families select answers to match those the audience selected. The host of the show usually says something like: "We polled 100 people, and asked them . . ." Then the feuding families have to come up with similar, or exact, answers. The closer they get to the answers that were most popular among the polled audience, the more points they get. If you polled 100 Craps players and asked them to tell you the best Craps system for winning at the game—unlike in the game show—you would get 100 different answers.

The reason is not only because there are that many, and more, Craps systems or strategies for winning, but also because Craps is such a highly subjective game. Each individual player is vastly different from all the others. If we were to give 10 Craps players exactly the same system or strategy for playing, we would get 10 vastly different results. This is because no two of these 10 players would play that same strategy the same way. Neither would they be equally as skilled, or equally as lucky. Skill and luck are both essential ingredients in any gambling, and particularly so for Craps. The skills are those developed through knowledge and the Keys to Winning. These are the skills of knowing when to bet, what to bet, how, and how much; learning to throw the dice and spot trends, learning discipline for yourself and your money, and learning the entire spectrum of the re- quired armament that any gambler should always possess before entering any casino for the purpose of gambling. Luck, on the other hand, is indefinable. Some people have it, and some don't. Most of us have a little bit of good luck, mixed in with a little bit of bad luck. That's life, and that's the way dem bones do roll. Therefore, for you to employ any method of play and succeed on a regular basis, even against what is always a negative expectation game, your skills armament must include not merely a strategy of play, but also the ability to recognize luck, and how that may re- quire you to deviate from your applied strategy.

What if your strategy calls for only the three bets that are the lowest house edge bets? What if you are making them perfectly, but aren't winning? What good is that strategy to you in that moment? Well, some experts would say, "It's a short terms trend, and these good bets will always over- come it in the long run." That is true. For games such as Blackjack, where your skills can actually turn a negative ex- pectation game into a player positive expectation game, this is even more true. But how long is "the long run"? In the universal scope of things, this could be billions of events before the trend finally turns. By that time your great-great- great-great-grandchildren may be rolling the dice on Mars.

The point is that while exploiting short-term trends is the only viable and essential means of winning on negative expectation games, in gambling in general, and in Craps in particular, holding steadfast to only that one method of play or strategy you have learned, contrary to what is actually happening in that short term, is disastrous. Your skills must also include the ability to know this, spot this, and deviate from any such applied strategy. Continuing with the above example, what if during that particular roll the shooter was rolling nothing but numbers and propositions, over and over and over again, and not making the point and not rolling a seven-out. I've seen this happen many times. I've seen shooters roll dice like this for 30 minutes, and more, at a time. It's very common, and if you hang out at the Craps tables for any length of time, you will see at least some of this happen with remarkable regularity. If this was the situation with you, then your two come bets—as part of your three-bet strategy—would be making money. But what of the other bets? Here, on this table and during that roll, your action should be on the propositions. That's where the money is to be made, under that specific circumstance. So, if you stick to your strategy, all the time without any flexibility, you will make some money, but not nearly as much as you could have. It is for reasons such as these that casinos don't lose as much money as they should have during monster rolls like these, and also why players lose money even during these rolls, or win only tiny amounts compared to what they could have won.

Therefore, an essential part of any strategy is to always remember that any such strategy is only one part of your overall skilled approach to the game. Strategies are usually flexible. They aren't designed as absolutes. Particularly for Craps, because this game is not only so volatile, but also highly subjective to each individual player. Skills in winning at Craps, and in all gambling, are not just the ability to learn the game and learn the strategy that you determine to be the best for your style of play, bankroll, and abilities. Skills in winning consistently also include your abilities to spot changes in the real-world occurrences, and be able to modify your strategy accordingly. Continuing with the above example, if you saw that this shooter was rolling all those propositions, then your immediate reaction should be to "try him out." This means to wager a small portion of your already acquired winnings—remember that this shooter is rolling numbers and therefore has rolled some of your come numbers for small wins already—on some of those long-shot high-house-edge propositions. Just because these bets are the "ugly" bets, doesn't mean that they never win. They do, and in this example, and in this circumstance, the major portion of your applied strategy is to recognize the deviation, and get on it. First, by that small test. Maybe $1, or whatever the table minimum bet may be, on each of the Hardways. Maybe a few tries at the field, or some of the other one-roll bets. But at least the Hardways. Maybe also include a "buy the 4 and 10." In this way, you would have understood what is happening and, at very minimal financial risk to you, have exploited the events as they were happening. If the situation continued, as with the example we are using here, then you would have won several of those small wagers, and could even have pressed. Now you would have had some serious money riding on the hot roll, and all of it as the result of small initial wagers used to first try, and then exploit, the statistical anomaly in the manner of this roll. This is how you can truly make powerful profits from Craps.

Even though in this instance the game still remains a negative expectation game, and you have deviated from the "safe" strategy to wagers that are among the highest house-edge bets in the game, nevertheless you have done so from the "cautious" player position, allowed for under the "skills" part of your knowledge of the game, and your abilities in wagering. In this case, we have used the example of the "conservative portfolio" player, the one whose majority of "investments" are always in the "safe" category. However, here you, as that example player, have also developed your observational and playing skills to a level that allowed you to "move" some of your investment to the highly risky portions of your Craps game portfolio, because your knowledge and game skills permitted you to spot the trend to the contrary statistical anomaly.

This is the same principle of "shifting assets" that allows Wall Street investors and stock analysts to move their money—or their client's money—into investment situations that others may have considered "risky" at the time, but failed to recognize the "trend" to the contrary accepted and established norm. Although such investment situations in the stock market likewise require at least a little bit of a gamble, so does everything in life. Stock analysts or investors who succeed do so because they have developed those skills that allow them to diminish their risk exposure even while "gambling" on "risky" ventures. In Craps, this is very similar, in fact almost identical. Craps "investment portfolios" mirror, to a remarkable degree, those same skills that allow such stock market players to succeed. While you may need millions, and even billions, of dollars to successfully play the stock market, in Craps you can not only develop those skills, but practice and apply them to financial benefits that can begin with a bankroll as low as a few hundred dollars.

The main point for all strategy play in Craps is that it is highly subjective to you, the player. Whatever knowledge you have acquired and retained, your skills, your abilities, your self-discipline, your financial status, all those, and the others listed throughout this book and in the Keys to Winning, all those are essential ingredients in your individual success in this game. Therefore, no matter what strategy you learn, how well you do with it is directly dependent on all those other factors that, collectively, make up who you are, and how good you are at the game. To make powerful profits from Craps is not just to make a bet and see what happens. This may work in some situations, and may be useful in some cases in Slots, or in games whose decisions are akin to a flip of the coin, but this will not work in Craps. Here, in this game, you must actually learn something, and then be able to manage the game as you play. Since I am a big baseball fan, I will use a baseball analogy:

Think of yourself as a Major League Baseball manager. You started as a kid in Little League. There, you learned what is what, what does what and how, and how to play. You then progressed as a player, and learned to master the game, the equipment, the rules, and all the different variables of the game, and its rules, as they all fluctuate during any given game. You learned to deal with adversity, such as rain, poor fields, bad umpiring, bad equipment, better teams, financial constraints, family, other players and their issues, and so on. You graduated to high school, then college, and finally you made it to the minor leagues as a player. Here, you quickly discovered that you just ain't that good as a player—but you also discovered that you *are* good as a manager. So, you took your first job as an assistant coach in A-Ball. To cut a long story short, you finally made it to the big leagues as a manager. Now, all your skills and experience have been acquired, and you are expected to make it all come together, and win. The skills you use to win are: knowledge of the game, patience, persistence, the ability to spot trends, the ability to modify your game plan as you see the game develop, the ability and skills to face adversity, skills to observe and adapt—well, you get the picture, I hope. These are all the same skills you need to win at Craps. The dice are like the baseball. The bets are like the players. The layout, and betting options, are like the ballfield. Now your skills as manager are to exploit the players and positions, and do it so you win.

I like analogies like this because they shed light on subjects that can be considered complex. Craps can easily be misunderstood as either a complex game or as a simple game. It can be both, depending on your abilities and skill level. So, in order to accommodate all readers, in this chapter I will present several Craps playing strategies, beginning with the simplest of strategies for Craps—the one that will make it possible for everyone to play, enjoy, and quite possibly win at this great game. Later, I will proceed to more and more complex playing and wagering strategies, each designed to build upon the one before. Together, these should provide you with as clear an approach to the game of Craps as I think is humanly possible. With these strategies, you will be empowered to play Craps as well, and as profitably, as the game allows. Later, in the next chapter, I will disclose what I have discovered is The Big Secret—a Craps method that I developed.

Now, let us begin with Craps strategies from the simplest, easiest to learn, and easiest to use.

A SIMPLE GAME

By far the simplest approach to Craps is one I mentioned earlier. Treat Craps as an "either-or" situation. Either the shooter will make winning rolls, or the shooter will not make winning rolls. This simple strategy requires you to only make a choice of two situations: Either bet the pass line, or bet the don't pass. Once you have made this decision, the rest is easy. In keeping with this being the *simple* strategy, I would here advise you not to even consider the don't pass as a betting option. If you do, it will become a little more complicated, but I will get into that in just a bit.

Once you have decided to bet the pass line, all your success now depends on the shooter rolling winning rolls. This means your pass line bets wins on the come out if the shooter rolls either a 7 or an 11. It will lose if the shooter rolls either a 2, 3, or 12. If none of these are rolled, this can only mean that a point has been established, and, therefore, the shooter rolled one of the following box numbers: 4, 5, 6, 8, 9, or 10. It is at this time that you should take at least single odds to back up your pass line wager. I would recommend double odds immediately, which will reduce the house edge on your combined pass line with odds bet to a mere 0.65 percent. Winning these bets will now depend on the shooter rolling the point number again before rolling any 7. If he does, you win. If he does not, you lose.

Now, after the point has been established, and before other rolls, you should make a come bet. If the shooter rolls a box number, your come bet now goes to that number. At this time, take double odds on that come number, similarly so to the pass line (yes, you can take only single odds, but take *at least* single odds, with my advice being double odds as a minimum). After the next roll, if there was no seven out, make another come bet, and repeat the procedure. When the next roll results in another box number, this second come bet goes on that number. Also back this with odds.

Here you have the simplest playing strategy for Craps. In this situation, you have three bets: Your original pass line bet, plus odds; then your two come bets, each with odds. If you have done this correctly, each of these bets will have the same base bet, and the same free odds. For example, let's assume that we are playing on a $5 minimum bet table, with a table maximum of $500, and offering 10x odds. These kinds of Craps games are offered in most casinos. This strategy requires you to make three wagers (assuming you will take at least the minimum of double odds, although you don't have to, since this strategy works almost as well with only single odds). I call this my "Three Bet Plan":

First bet: $5 original pass line wager, plus $10 in free
   odds
Second bet: $5 original come bet, plus $10 in free odds
   ($15 on 6 or 8, if allowed)
Third bet: $5 second come bet, plus $10 in free odds
   ($15 on 6 or 8, if allowed)

   This gives you $45 in total action ($50 if one come is either a 6 or an 8, or $55 if both come numbers are either the
6 or the 8, and if the casino allows you the higher odds
wager). Your original pass line bet with double odds exposes you to a mere 0.65 percent house edge. Each of the
two come bets, with double odds, exposes you to a mere
0.61 percent house edge. Here, in this simplest of all Craps
strategies, you have made the most beneficial group of wagers that are possible in the game, exposing yourself to the
least statistical risk. This is the easiest, and "safest," strategy play available in this game.
   Of course, you could have done this on the dark side. In
that case, you would have chosen to bet that the shooter
will not make winning rolls—as previously stated, the exact
opposite to the above description. If this was your "either-
or" choice, you would have done the opposite to the above.
You would have put your original bet on the don't pass line,
then bridged it with $20 in free odds to win $10 (or whatever the odds may be relative to the point). You then would
have made two don't come bets, and bridge each with the
appropriate odds, wagering more to win less. Now, winning
will depend on the shooter rolling any 7 before rolling the
point or either of your don't come bets. This strategy exposes you to slightly lower house edge on these bets, but so
slightly to make this statistically insignificant. This strategy
is not very useful if all you are trying to do is to learn the
simplest method to get into the game, and make some good
value bets. But, since this is also nearly as simple as the

pass line alternative, yes, you can do this. Just remember that if you do, you have to bet more to win less. To me, that's not a good idea for a strategy at this stage of your development as a skilled Craps strategy player. Best advice—stick to the three bets shown earlier, for the front line play. It will be easier on your mind, and easier on your wallet. It will make you more money, and cost you less.

HEDGING BETS

The next step up from the above simple strategy is a method of play called "hedging." This requires a little more familiarity with the game, but is in actuality a very simple method of attempting to cover the converse negative occurrences against primary wagered events. Although practiced by many Craps players, the reality is that hedging your bets exposes you to a greater house edge and, therefore, often defeats the purpose for which such bets were made. It is, nevertheless, a part of any strategy to at least consider the viability of such play. Under some circumstances, hedging may in fact prove to be a viable method. First, however, let us explore what it is, and why it is—statistically—inadvisable under the majority of circumstances.

Hedging a bet simply means that, in addition to your original bet, you also make another bet, or bets, which is designed to give you a pay in the event that a loss occurs on your primary bet. The most common example of "hedging" is betting the C&E on the come out roll, in addition to a pass line wager. It works like this: First, you make a pass line bet of, say, $5. This is traditionally the minimum bet allowed in the majority of major casinos. So, now you have the opportunity to win $5 if the shooter rolls either a 7 or an 11 on the very next roll; if the shooter rolls a point, then the outcome depends on whether the point is rolled before any 7. This is the same kind of example as that shown immediately above, with the "Three Bet Plan." However, on the come out roll, your pass line bet loses if any 2, 3, or 12 is rolled. To "hedge" the pass line bet against the possibility of losing it if a 2, 3, or 12 is rolled, many players will bet Any Craps in addition to the pass line wager. The Any Craps bet is a one-roll proposition, and wins if any 2, 3, or 12 is rolled immediately on the next roll. Therefore, when making the $5 pass line wager, players often add an extra $1 bet on the Any Craps.

Any Craps will traditionally pay 7:1, and faces a house edge of around 11 percent. So, if on the very next roll—which in this case is the come out roll—the shooter happens to roll either the 2, 3, or 12, then the $5 pass line bet automatically loses. But, the player who had also made the $1 Any Craps wager will now be paid $7. So, the player has risked a total of $6—the $5 pass line bet plus the $1 Any Craps bet—and now has received $7 back, for a profit of $1. In addition, the player can also take back the $1 bet, which is still on the Any Craps bet. This does not have to ride on the next roll, even though the next roll is another come out roll. You can actually take that bet down, and so you would have a gross of $8 returned to you, for an overall profit of $2. Of course, in casinos where you only get paid 7 *for* 1, you would only gross $7, for an overall profit of $1. This is one of the major reasons why playing Craps on tables where the pays are "for 1" is really not a good idea at all.

So, as you can see, this player has made a $2 profit by hedging the pass line bet with an extra $1 bet on the Any Craps. Most players who practice this form of bet hedging will actually also bet the Yo—the Eleven—along with the Any Craps. That's why there's a space on the table layout called the C&E, which stands for a wager on any craps *and* 11. This also faces a house edge of around 11 percent, and wins if any craps—the 2, 3, or 12—is rolled on the next roll, or if the 11 is so rolled, and lose otherwise. If the 11 is rolled, the player wins the pass line bet, plus is paid at 15:1 for the 11 (or the worse pay of 15-1, in which case I hope you are no longer playing Craps in that casino, or on that table). For the $5 pass line bet, this hedge now produces a win of $5 on the pass line, plus a win of $15 on the 11 (at 15:1). Both the pass line $5 wager and the $1 on the 11 are still left, but the $1 on the Any Craps is lost. So, this player now has a gross of $5 + $5 + $1 − $1 + $15 = $25 total. This is an overall profit of $18, when we deduct the original $5 pass line bet, the $1 bet on Any Craps which was lost, and the $1 original bet on the Yo.

So far so good. So what is the problem with this strategy? First, you lose both the bets on the C&E when a 7 is rolled on the come out roll. Continuing with the $5 pass line example, and assuming a hedge bet of $1 each on the C&E (which is traditionally mandatory in most major casinos), even though the $5 pass line bet wins when any 7 is rolled, now your hedge bets lose. So, instead of gaining a $5 profit, you now have a $5 gross, minus the $2 loss, for a net profit of only $3. You just gave up 40 percent of your expected profit on that bet! Continuing with the same example, what if a 4, 5, 6, 8, 9, or 10 were the roll? Well, since this was a come out roll, this now means that the point was established. Whatever the point, both your C&E bets now lost. In addition, your $5 pass line bet now can win only if the point is rolled again, before any 7. What did the come out hedge do for you?

By betting C&E on the come out, you "hedged" a good bet with a bad one. The C&E faces a house edge of 12.5 percent, and its combined pay is at 13:3, versus the true odds of 15:3. You have hedged what is a low house edge bet—1.4 percent for the pass line bet—by betting on events that face an 11 percent house edge. On the come out, you win when any 7 is rolled. You therefore have six ways to win by the roll of any 7, each of which causes both your C&E bets to lose. This costs you about 40 percent of your winnings on these events. You have only two ways in which to win both the pass line bets and the Yo, by the roll of an 11. But, you lose the Any Craps portion of your C&E bet. You can win the Any Craps only if a 2, 3, or 12 are rolled. A 2 can only be rolled one way. A 12 can only be rolled one way. A 3 can only be rolled two ways. So, your Any Craps can only win a combined four ways. But whenever any of the Any Craps numbers so win for your hedge, this means you have lost the original pass line bet. Include the 11, and your C&E bet can only win a combined six ways—four ways to roll Any Craps, and two ways to roll an 11. This is the same number of ways in which any 7 can be rolled, but remember that if any 7 is rolled, although your pass line bets wins, your C&E bets lose. And if Any Craps wins, then your pass line bet and the 11 bet both lose. So, your only profitable situation is when an 11 is rolled, and this can only happen two times out of each 36 rolls, statistically speaking.

It's plain to see that you can lose both the C&E hedge bets more frequently than any wins on them can justify their worth. Therefore, they really aren't "hedge" bets at all. They are house bets, which make more money for the house, and less for the player. Although they may appear interesting and, to the uninitiated, as a good "hedge" bet, they are far from it, as understood within the statistical model. Overall, if you make C&E hedge bets on each come out roll, you will be costing yourself about 20 percent of your overall profits (allowing for those two in 36 events when you win on the 11), and face a house edge much higher than if you simply made the low house edge pass line bet, without any "hedge," and then just played the game in accordance with the first Three Bet Plan, as shown above. Adding the "hedge" to your wagering strategy may look inviting, and may appear logical, but it is actually very costly when understood within the statistical model. However, this doesn't mean that it is always inadvisable. Based on your skills in the game, as you advance and as you will discover later in this chapter, there may indeed be occasions where such hedge bets may be of value. This will depend entirely on your ability to judge the game. If, for example, you think that the shooter may roll craps, and is therefore a cold shooter, or that there's cold dice or a cold table, whatever your skills in observational analysis may be, you may consider such hedge bets.

If this is so, however, my question would be, "Why?" If you have spotted this trend toward negative rolls, why would you then still be on the pass line, and hedge your bets? If you are that good in Craps, wouldn't you instead immediately start betting against the shooter? Your action should then immediately be shifted to the "don't" side, and your bets should be darksided. This would make a whole lot more sense if you started out as a frontliner and the game suddenly turned, for however long that trend may be. In my opinion, any "hedging" seems a waste of money and effort. I guess the only way when it would make some sense would be if the shooter was hot, and you wanted to exploit the 11 as the one roll proposition, and then chose to add the Any Craps "just in case." There could be an argument made for this strategy. However, to keep things simple, my simplest advise would be to avoid hedging your bets, no matter what. It simply isn't worth it, if you do it in this manner, and especially on the come out roll. Of course, this doesn't exclude the group bet situations, whereby multiple bets are used to exploit the roll. But these aren't "hedge" bets in the same sense.

Making hedge bets after the point has been established is also a practice that some players are prone to teach to those who may be new to the game, or don't know any better. These players will often bet the Any 7 as a hedge against the sudden appearance of that dreaded number, when you are a frontliner with some numbers spread. Mostly, this is done after the shooter has rolled for a while, and these players think "it's about time" that the 7 showed up. It's a lousy bet. The action mirrors that of hedging on the come out roll with a bet on C&E. Here, you are betting that $1 (or whatever amount, relative to your overall spread of bets) that the next roll will be that 7, expecting a 4:1 payoff. This bet faces a house edge of 16.67 percent, and more than 18 percent in those casinos that will only pay you at 4-1, while the true odds are 6:1. If you have a $5 pass line bet with double odds, plus two come bets each with double odds, you have a risk of $45 total, as in the earlier example (or slightly higher if your odds are higher on the 6 and/or 8, also as shown earlier). At 4:1 payoff, you would have to hedge bet the Any 7 for $12, for a total of $48 payoff if you hit it, in order to assure yourself of a $3 profit (higher bet if you took higher odds on 6 and 8, or if you are in a casino paying only 4-1). Otherwise, any lower hedge bet will assure you of a loss no matter what happened. So, assuming the best possible outcome, your $12 hedge bet wins. Your $45 in pass line and come bets with odds now lose, and your Any 7 wins, for a total of $48, a profit of $3 over your original $45 combined bets; plus you get the $12 back. You risked a total of $45 + $12 = $57, and received a total gross of $48 + $12 = $60, for that total net profit of $3. In effect, you risked $57 to win $3, with only a 6 in 36 shot at making it. Think about it. Exactly how is this a good bet? Risking $57 to win $3 on one roll? Some hedge!

The point is the same as for the popular hedge on the come out roll. While it looks inviting, and sounds good when it is talked during the game, the real-world truth is plainly that you are hedging what is essentially a good bet by adding what is actually a very lousy bet. Combined, the house will eat you up, and it won't even take any "long term" to do this. Even in just an hour of playing this way, you will lose more than you win. This, therefore, defeats the purpose of betting the low house edge pass line and come bets with odds (or their dark side cousins). Is there a time to make a hedge bet? Yes, it's possible. But only on the come out, if you must. When? Call me when the moon turns pink.

PASS LINE AND PLACE THE 6 AND 8

Another method of Craps strategy is a modification of the pass line and two come bets, which I called the Three Bet Plan. This one is also a Three Bet Plan, and like the one mentioned earlier, it is also statistically among the best strategies to use in Craps. Start by making a pass line bet, and then follow it up with two place bets on the 6 and the 8. If either the 6 or the 8 is the point, then you can either not make another place bet and wait for the results, or you can place the 5 or the 9 to give you the three bets. Normally, however, it is better to simply place the 6 and the 8, or only the other if one is the point, and forego the additional bet. Continuing with the example established above, and using the $5 minimum wager, here's how this strategy works out:

First, make the $5 pass line bet. After the point is established, instead of making a come bet, and then another, now just immediately place the 6 and the 8. At this time, we will here assume that the point is something other than either the 6 and/or the 8. If the point isn't either the 6 or the 8, then what the point actually is doesn't matter for the sake of this example. Since both the 6 and the 8 pay off at 7:6, each place bet on these numbers must be in increments of $6. In this example, I would recommend that you immediately start with a $12 bet on both the 6 and the 8. This is akin to the come bet with odds, as in the earlier strategy example. By making the pass line bet, then backing it up with odds, and then making two come bets, and backing each of these with odds, you will have the average $45 exposed on that roll (more if either or both of these come bets land on the 6 and the 8, but that was already discussed).

By placing the 6 and the 8 for $12 each, and having the pass line bet with double odds, you now have a total of $39 exposed on this roll. This is a total of $6 less than the pass line plus two come bets strategy. Your pass line bet with double odds now faces a house edge of a mere 0.65 percent, while each of your place bets on the 6 and the 8 face the small house edge of 1.5 percent. This method of betting, therefore, allows you to risk less then the earlier Three Bet Plan, while still facing a relative small house edge. Viewed from the statistical model, this is a slightly better playing strategy than the earlier Three Bet Plan. This can be extended further in the event that the point is either the 6 or the 8. Anytime the point is either the 6 or the 8, your front line bets have the most chance of success, as indeed do the come bets on either of these two numbers, or your place bets. This is because each of these two numbers—6 and 8—can be rolled five ways, while the dreaded 7 can only be rolled six ways. So, statistically, the numbers 6 and 8 are only slightly an underdog against the 7.

If the point turns out to be either the 6 or the 8, then you can let your two bets stand as they are. In that case, you now have only two bets riding. The $5 pass line bet and double odds ($15 total), plus the place bet on either the 6 or the 8, whichever one is not the point, for the $12. This gives you a total of $27 exposed on that roll, still on bets facing the lowest house edge. Of course, you can choose to add another place bet to make the complete Three Bet Plan. If you do, then your only option should be either the 5 or the 9. Both will cost you a minimum of $5 as a place bet. In accordance with the strategy plan for this example, I would recommend a $10 wager on either the 5 or the 9 in case either the 6 or the 8 is the point. Don't, however, wager on *both* the 5 and the 9. That would give you four bets, and this would defeat the purpose of the simplicity of this Three Bet Plan. By placing either the 5 or the 9 as your third bet, this will expose you to a total wager of $15 on the pass line ($5 + $10 double odds) + $12 on either the 6 or the 8 (whichever one is not the point) + $10 on either the 5 or the 9 (whichever you choose) = $37. This is still a lower total exposure than the earlier Three Bet Plan on the pass line and two come bets, where the total exposure was $45 as the base. However, your 5 and/or 9 now faces a house edge of 4 percent, and this therefore makes this second Three Bet Plan variation a higher risk. Even though you are wagering slightly less than the pass line plus two come bets strategy, here you are now exposing your wagers to a higher possibility of loss, statistically speaking.

Nevertheless, both of these options are a viable method of playing Craps to the greatest statistical benefit. By betting the pass line with double odds, and then placing the 6 and the 8 for $12 each as the starting point, or placing either the 6 or the 8 if one is the point and then adding as the third bet either the 5 or the 9, this still provides you with the best methods of obtaining the most frequent wins while facing the lowest possible house edge, statistically speaking. Each of these three versions of the Three Bet Plan is eminently workable, in my way of understanding and speaking. As I mentioned earlier, I often seek to understand casino games, and exploit their profitability, based on the "workability" principle, rather than the statistical model. In these cases, it just so happens that the statistical model fits neatly into the workability principle. For those reasons, if not any others, approaching your Craps playing strategy by employing either of these three methods provides you with a solid foundation for Craps profits. As your knowledge and mastery of the game improve, you will then be able to build on this strategy. Whatever else you add to it will become stronger because of it, since this is the solid foundation of such practical thinking when it comes to exploiting the game for powerful profits. Even if, later, you decide to use some of the more "risky" strategies, even then your game plan will be vested in a solid beginning, if you understand these principles of wagering, and why they are profitable.

PLACE BET CRITICS

Using place bets on the 6 and the 8 as part of a front line Craps playing strategy, as described immediately above, is one of the more statistically successful methods of playing the game. Adding additional place bets can be a further refinement of this strategy. However, making place bets as opposed to come bets does have its critics. I am going to relate to you a situation of place bet criticism that happened to catch my eye in a recent issue of a gaming publication. Although this particular form of place bet criticism isn't unique to the author of that particular article, it does capture the essence of why some authors and gaming experts tend to criticize place bets as a prominent part of any Craps playing strategy.

This particular article was written by Alan Krigman, and was published in the June 11–June 17, 2002, issue of the Las Vegas newspaper *Gaming Today*. I wish to stress at the outset that my comments are aimed at the method of criticism of the place bet strategies as explained in Alan's article, and *not* of Alan himself. I have absolutely no bone to pick with him nor any desire to criticize him or any of his writings. I just happened to pick up his version of this argument, and am using it here because he did such a great job of explaining the positions. I hope my arguments will be understood as being made against the *theory* being espoused, and *not* against the man who happened to write this article.

The argument is a percentage differential between successes of using come bets as part of your Craps playing strategy, versus making place bets. In the Recommended Reading section at the end of this book, I will tell you how you can obtain a copy of this article. You can easily locate it and read it for yourself. The question being asked is, simply: Is it better to make come bets or place bets? According to the theory being proposed by the place bet critics, as demonstrated in that article, come bets have a profit success ratio of 49.29 percent, versus the place bet success ratio of only 45.45 percent for the 6 and the 8, 40 percent for the 5 and the 9, and 33.33 percent for the 4 and the 10. Based on this analysis, making come bets is more advantageous than place bets, even if the come bet has to hit twice to pay off. And that's where the rub is in this argument. You see, proponents of place bets as a better alternative—of which I am one—tend to argue that one of the main reasons why a place bet is a better alternative to come bets is because the place bet only has to hit once to win, while the come bet has to hit twice: First after you make the come bet, when it goes on that come number, and second, to hit that come number again before any 7 to win. It seems logical.

The critics, however, point out that this can easily be considered as "pseudo logic," because the percentages clearly show that the come bet is a better alternative. As shown earlier, the come bets win a combined 49.29 percent, while the best of the place bets, those on the 6 and the 8, only win a combined 45.45 percent. Okay, so how can this be? Well, the basis for this argument is that the come bet wins whenever the 7 or the 11 are rolled immediately after the bet is made in the come bet area. This, therefore, provides for the "extra" percentage differential over the place bets. Place bets are made directly on the numbers, and, therefore, cannot win if the very next roll is either the 7 or the 11. Okay, so far so good. However—what this theory fails to take into account is the fact that the come bets also lose whenever a 2, 3, or 12 are rolled immediately after the come bet is made in the come bet area. The come bet wins in the come bet area if either a 7 or an 11 is rolled immediately after the come bet is made, but loses if a 2, 3, or 12 is so rolled. This is, seemingly, conveniently forgotten by those who claim such a statistical advantage for come bets versus place bets. There are six ways to roll any 7, and two ways to roll an 11, so the come bet in the come bet area has an eight in 36 chance of winning on the next roll. [The 2 can be rolled only one way, the 12 can be rolled only one way, and the 3 can be rolled two ways, so this same come bet has a four in 36 chance of losing.]

Now, of course, we have to add the possibility that *neither* the 2, 3, 7, 11, nor 12 is rolled immediately after the come bet is made. That can only mean that one of the box numbers was rolled, meaning either 4, 5, 6, 8, 9, or 10. There are three ways to roll a 4 or 10, four ways to roll a 5 or 9, and five ways to roll a 6 or 8. This equals 24 ways to roll a come number, meaning that the come bet has an eight ways in 36 to win immediately on the next roll, four ways in 36 to immediately lose on the next roll, and 24 ways in 36 to land on a box number. But when it lands on a box number, that number then has to be rolled again in order for it to win. Now the odds are different. If the come bet landed on the 4 or the 10, it now has only a three in 36 chance of winning, while a six in 36 chance of losing. If it lands on the 5 or the 9, it has a four in 36 chance to win, and six in 36 chance to lose. If it lands on the 6 or the 8, it has the best chance of all to win, being a five in 36 chance to win, while a six in 36 chance to lose. Because the come has to be rolled twice to actually win, it is exposed to the odds *against two* times! First, on the come bet, where it will lose if a 2, 3, or 12 is lost. Then, if it lands on a box number, it is exposed to that number's odds of losing, versus the short odds of winning, based on whatever number it so landed. Its exposure to a combined loss, therefore, invalidates the assumption of a percentage differential benefit, versus place bets that only need to hit once. Place bets are exposed to their statistical losses only once. Come bets are exposed to such statistical losses twice. Even though the loss-exposure is somewhat compensated for by the fact that the come bet wins four times more often than it loses (eight ways to win and four ways to lose on the very next roll after the come bet is first made), this doesn't compensate for the fact that the come bet will be exposed to its number's loss potential again, thus defeating the compensating factor of the lower loss frequency immediately after it was made.

To recap: the theory of place bet criticism states that come bets have a combined better odds of winning than place bets, by a factor of 49.29 percent versus 45.45 percent for the 6 and the 8, 40 percent for the 5 and the 9, and 33.33 percent for the 4 and the 10. However, when you factor into this equation the fact that the come bet is exposed twice to potential losses, and then has to be rolled twice in order to provide a financial benefit (the win), it turns out that the fractional ratio between the come bets and the place bets is statistically insignificant. Also, consider this: One of my three versions of the Three Bet Plan was the one where we make two place bets on the 6 and the 8, in addition to the pass line bet with odds. Odds wise, these are three of the best bets, exposing the least financial risk ($37 versus $45 for the come bets plan), while facing the combined lowest house edge possible for these bets. Although the come bets face a slightly lower house edge, due to the free odds available on these bets, the place bets don't face twice the loss exposure to the initial bet. They can *not lose* even if the next roll immediately after they are made is either the 2, the 3, or the 12, all rolls that lose for the original come bet. While they don't win on the rolls of 7 or 11, conversely they don't have to be rolled twice before any 7. What if one player makes a come bet, and another a place bet on 6, and the very next roll is a 6? The come player's bet is put on the 6, at which time he should take the odds. However, the place player's bet has already won. What if the next roll was a 7? Well, then, both the come player and the place player have lost their bet on the 6, and both lost their pass line bets with odds. But, who has more money? Well, the place player, because his place bet on the 6 hit. Just once, but that was enough. And that's why the theory of come bets being more favorable, statistically speaking, leaks like a rusty bucket.

The plain truth is that both methods of playing Craps are good bets. Betting the come bets with the pass line, as the frontliner's Three Bet Plan #1, is a good way to play the game. Betting the pass line and then placing two numbers, the 6 and the 8 preferably, is equally as good. This is the Three Bet Plan #2. If the point is either the 6 or the 8, so much the better for both the pass line bets. Now, the place player can place either the 5 or the 9, and thus have three bets riding. This is the Three Bet Plan #3. Only in this instance does the place player have a very slightly lower expectation of a win, and that is due to the fact that the 5 and the 9 face a higher house edge as place bets, versus being achieved as come bets. Otherwise, the actual percentages are virtually the same.

Further, consider this. Even according to the theory, and let's here assume that the critics of place betting are correct (which they aren't), the statistical difference between the place bets on the 6 and the 8—the Three Bet Plan #2—face only a 3.8 percentage differential between that theory's estimate of a combined 49.29 percent success ratio for the come bets, versus the 45.45 percent ratio for the place 6 and 8. Even if that theory were correct, this small a percentage differential is statistically minute. In the very short term of your exposure to the Craps game, it simply wouldn't make any financial difference. The object is to *win money* at Craps. The object is *not* to wager simply to verify the statistics. And that's the final failure of any such theory against the place player's strategy. It is the *financial gain that matters,* and *not* the statistical differential. As we have seen, the actual reality is that both the come bets and the place bets on 6 and 8 are statistically identical. Where the theory has its greatest advantage is only fractionally on the place bets of 5 and 9, and much more so for place bets on 4 and 10. While the placing of the 5 and the 9 may be overcome by the single-hit requirement, and by the fact that these place bets should only be used as part of the Three Bet Plan #3 strategy, as a side option in the event that the point is either the 6 or the 8, placing the 4 and the 10 is *never* an option. At least not for anyone who knows something about Craps. Why would anyone do this, when placing the 4 and the 10 exposes your bets to a 6.67 percent house edge, while buying the 4 and the 10 for at least $25 each lowers this to about a 4.8 percent house edge. Pushing the house to accept buy wagers of $35, $38, or $39 on the 4 and the 10 further reduces the house edge to about 2.8 percent, as we have discussed earlier. So, why factor the 4 and the 10 into the come bets versus the place bets at all? No place player would ever place the 4 and the 10, so that argument is totally moot. This is the fourth reason why the theory of the lower-value win-expectation for the place player fails.

If you add all these other factors into the equation, you will find that the place player would only place the 6 and the 8, in addition to his pass line bet with odds, and only place either the 5 or the 9 if either the 6 or the 8 happened to be the point. He would never place the 4 and the 10. Even if he placed both the 5 and the 9, he would still not be so far away from the come player's win-expectation percentage as to be considered anything other than statistically near, if not identical. In any such situation, the reality happens to be that the financial gain versus the percentage differential is also almost the same. While the come player wins the come bet with free odds, if he wins the come bet, the place player wins that place bet *twice* during these events. Assuming that the place player has placed the 6 and the 8 immediately after the come out roll established the point, and at the same time as the come player made the come bet, the place player will already win once when the come player lands on the number. While the come player will then be able to take odds, the place player can press the bet. So, if the number hits again, the come player will win his bet plus odds, while the place player will win twice the place bet amount, still having won twice versus the place player's single win. If you add it all up, it turns out that the differences in financial benefits to either player are about the same. While the place player will risk less at the outset, overall he will win a little less if the place numbers hit twice and he doesn't press, because the come player will be paid his odds wager in addition to the original come bet. But if the place player presses the win, he will then have $24 on the number with only a $12 investment, and if the number hits again to make that come player's win the first time, now the place player will win again, and be able to take down his bet with a double-amount win. In actuality, these financial benefits versus their combined risk are also almost identical, with a differential of only about $7 for the base bets, higher for the odds bets and potential press bets for the place player. If we toss out the variables, and deal only with the base wagers, then the financial benefits are virtually equal for each player. So, in the final analysis, neither the come player nor the place player gains anything over the other, in accordance with either Three Bet Plan strategy.

The differences are simply too small to be a factor, either

in the immediate, or the long term. I hope this helps to clarify the theoretical criticism sometimes employed against the place player, by trying to show that come players have a small edge. In one sense they do, if we think that place players would ever place the 4 and the 10. No place player worth his salt would ever do that, so that's enough, and the argument fails right there and then. And that, dear friends, should be enough about this.

PASS, PLACE, AND BUY (GROUP BETS)

Here I am going to suggest a strategy that builds upon those stated earlier. As with all of these so far, these are front line strategies, vested in the right-way bets *with* the shooter. I have already briefly touched upon the don't side, and although I will again mention the dark side a little later in this strategy chapter, most of what I will recommend as your better strategy choices will fall into the frontliner category. I have already stated my reasons for such thinking, so from here on, I won't mention the differences any further.

This strategy portion will consist of what I call the Four Bet Plan and the Six Bet Plan. Each of these is the natural outgrowth from those listed above. While each of the Three Bet Plans shown earlier were firmly vested in the "safe" portion of your Craps investment portfolio, as far as the traditionally understood statistics are concerned, these Four and Six Bet Plans are more in the "speculative" portion of your Craps portfolio. However, they are not "aggressive" bets, because these are still vested in the principle of minimizing risk exposure and house edge. Each of these group wagers consists of the best bets to make, statistically speaking, while adding a more "adventurous" portion to the overall betting strategy. As I mentioned earlier, these fall into the category of "group wagers," or "group bets." The reason

why the earlier Three Bet Plans were not considered as
"group bets" is not that they aren't groups, which they are,
but because each of these bets *individually* faces only the
minimum house edge among all of the available Craps bets.
Since each of the bets in the Three Bet Plans can easily be
made just as effectively alone, without the requirement of
being grouped with the others, they aren't in that same
sense a "group bet," as will be the case with these wagers
we are about to explore. Here we are now going to add that
element of increased risk exposure, and that's why they are
more firmly classified in the "group" bet category. Individually, only some parts are the statistically better bets, while
their more "adventurous" parts would, or should, not be tried
individually due to these individual bets' overall greater exposure to a higher house edge.

I will begin with the Four Bet Plan. This will consist of
a pass line bet with at least double odds, plus three place
bets. Continuing with the earlier established example of the
minimum $5 wager, this wagering strategy consists of mak-
ing at least the $5 pass line bet, then backing this up with at
least double odds ($10 minimum), and then placing three
additional bets on the 6, 8, and either the 5 or the 9. If the
point is either the 6 or the 8, then you would place the
other, plus the 5 and the 9. Let's assume here that the point
is 6. You will then back up your front line bet with double
odds ($15 in many casinos), and then place the 8 for $12,
and the 5 and the 9 for $10 each. You will now have a total
of $47 exposed (assuming the availability of the higher odds
bet for the front line free odds in the case of the point being
either the 6 or the 8; if neither the 6 nor the 8 was the point,
then your exposure would be the $10 free odds instead of
$15, leaving a total of $42 as your overall wager risk).

In this strategy, you have covered the point (in this example the 6) with the pass line wager plus odds, exposing
yourself to a mere 0.65 percent house edge on this bet, then

placed the 8 (remember, in this example the point is the 6) for a total of $12, exposing that wager to a mere 1.5 percent house edge. You then also placed the 5 and the 9 for $10 each, exposing each of these bets to the house edge of 4 percent. You have now made four wagers as a group, with one of them being under one percent house edge, the second under 2 percent house edge, and the other two at the higher exposure of the 4 percent house edge. Although we do understand that each of these is an independent mathematical event, if viewed as a *group*—in accordance with the workability principle for conceptual perspectives for financial gains in the game—we have a combined exposure of 0.65 percent + 1.52 percent + 4 percent + 4 percent divided by 4 bets = a combined house edge exposure of a mere 2.54 percent. Please understand that this is merely a manner of understanding our approach to these wagers as a group.

This method of illustrating the group-event will not alter, nor diminish, the individual house edge exposures of each individual bet that is part of this group. However, since we are trying to master a wagering strategy for the purpose of making some powerful profits, it behooves us to consider this Four Bet Plan as a single wager. If so considered, at our own choice, then we can calculate the perceptual house edge we are facing, when we add all those four separate bets together and view them as a single wager. This, then, shows us that we have a reasonable wager overall as that group, even though we are facing what is essentially a pretty high house edge on the combined group. However, as we have stated earlier, the objective here is not so much to reduce the house edge on these combined group bets, but to maximize the profit potential by using the diminished risk capacity model I introduced much earlier in this book. This method of wagering is, as stated, most definitely in the "more aggressive" portion of your Craps playing investment portfolio, and therefore it is essential that you understand this portion of the strategy advice for what it is—a *further-ing of the aggressiveness in your betting.*

The farther we get into the more "aggressive" style wa-gering strategies, the more risky they will be and the higher their combined house edge will grow as a group, since many of these bets will be, individually, among the higher house edge bets in the game. But that is the purpose of ad-vancing these playing strategies, because it is our intent to *maximize the financial gain.* As mentioned earlier, finan-ciers and stock market operatives must employ risky invest-ments as part of their overall portfolio stratagies, because without this their funds would lag so far behind their com-petitors' that they would lose their clients. So, to do this, as we have shown for the Craps version of this approach, these investment professionals divide their total portfolios into the categories of the "safe," the "adventurous," and the "ag-gressive." This is precisely what we are doing here with these strategy plans for Craps, and the approach, and analy-sis, is the same. Therefore, don't suddenly become afraid when considering these group bets. They will get more and more risky, but their rewards will get more and more prof-itable. By combining these into the group plans I am indi-cating, you will be able to gain the maximum benefits while risking the minimum financial exposure and the lowest combined house edge against such groups possible. When applied, by you, through your own study of the game, and the information in this book as a whole, you will be empow-ered to select whichever strategy best fits your personality, knowledge, skills, abilities, goals, objectives, and bankroll. That's why I am taking this graduated approach to explor-ing these methods of playing Craps—from the simplest and safest, through the mildly aggressive, all the way to the fully speculative, but vested in an overall understanding of rela-tive group risk versus gain, within both the workability principle, and the diminished risk capacity model.

Under this Four Bet Plan, you have the best of the best, along with what is essentially a "medium" house bet, these being the place bets on the 5 and the 9. If the point is 8 as opposed to the 6 in this example, then the same applies exactly. If the point is either the 5 or the 9, then your wagers are place bets on the 6 and the 8 at at least $12 each, and $10 on the 5 or the 9, whichever is not the point. You still have four bets working: the pass line, which plays on whatever is the point, plus the place bets on the other three numbers—5, 6, 8, or 9, with one of these being the point. If the point is either the 4 or the 10, then you have Five Bets, and that's why I will call this the Five Bet Plan Differential (FBPD for short). Now, and only if the point is the 4 or the 10, you will have the pass line bet that plays on the point, and then four place bets, one each on the 5, 6, 8, and 9. You now have a total exposure of $59, facing a combined group house edge of 2.34 percent. Still within the reasonably acceptable risk formula. Again, remember that this combined house edge factor is merely an indicator of our choice to view these bets as a single group wager. Nothing changes for the individual number odds. Now we win if either the 5, 6, 8, 9, or the point is rolled. Since either the 4 or the 10 is here the point, in this situation, this means that we can win the pass line bet if the 4 or the 10 is rolled (whichever is the point), and we win the place bets on the 6, 8, 5, and 9 as long as the shooter rolls these numbers before rolling any 7. There are three ways to roll the 4 or the 10, so let us assume here that the 4 is the point. Now we have a 3 in 36 chance of winning on the pass line, by rolling the point-4 before any 7. Not too good, by itself, when either the 4 or the 10 are the point. But we have a group bet, so what about the other winning potentials? Well, we have four ways to roll the 5 and the 9, and five ways to roll the 6 and the 8, so this gives us a total of 18 ways in 36 to roll a winner on these placed numbers. If the point is 4, only a roll of 10 or 7 will result in a no win for us. This strategy gives us a total of 21 ways out of 36 to roll a winner. Winning the $12 bet on the 6 and/or 8 will immediately pay us at 7:6, while winning on the 5 and/or 9 will pay us at 7:5. Rolling the point will pay us at 2:1 on the free odds and 1:1 for the original pass line bets, and we don't lose any of the place bets. Either way you slice it, risking a combined perceived house edge of 2.34 percent on this group bet, and having a 21 in 36 chance to roll a winner over the combined group, provides for some hefty wins under the best circumstances these bets can allow in the game of Craps. If the shooter rolls just two of the place numbers, we have a nice win. Very often the shooter will keep rolling numbers, and even if he eventually craps out, this method of playing Craps will combine to provide a very profitable result.

Now to the Six Bet Plan. Here we are most definitely getting into the "aggressive" portions of our playing portfolio. The main reason why this Six Bet Plan is considered an "aggressive" strategy is because it not only involves the risk of more money, but it also exposes you to some of the higher house edge bets. There's also a third reason, and this may be even more profound for some players—this strategy exposes you to a much greater financial risk. You will have to put more of your money on the table, as a whole, covering the group bet. You will actually have six total bets riding on each roll of the dice, and that's why it's called the Six Bet Plan. Although this strategy is still among the best and easiest methods of making Craps bets for substantial profits, the further we go increasing not only the number of total bets exposed on any individual roll of the dice, but also the total financial risk, the more bankroll we will need, and the higher the risk of ruin if we happen to choose badly, or run into one of those inevitable anomalies that will result in several dice rolls contrary to even the expected statistical occurrences. It is important to remember that the "aggressive" part of this strategy means just that—you will be far more prone to financial fluctuations in your fortune. This means you must have the necessary bankroll to be able to sustain the play. It also means you must be a lot more aware of what is happening on the table. Once you start getting involved in betting strategies like this one, you will now more than ever have to pay close attention to the rolls the shooters are making. As we continue to expand the realm of our "risky" action, we will be making higher profits per result, but we are also exposed to higher cumulative losses. Therefore, it is at these times when the skills of knowing when to call bets "off" or "down" come specifically into focus. Also, this is the time when you will have to be very conscious of just how well the dice are passing.

With the Six Bet Plan strategy, you may have to shift your bets to the dark side if the shooters, and/or dice, turn cold. With the added exposure of your bets, like in this plan, your profitability will be increased by your abilities to spot negative trends and shift your wagers from the front line to the dark side as the game demands, and then back again. This also means you will have to be able to modify your wagering structure to accommodate such shifts. All of this can only be done by you, based upon your knowledge of the game and your skills in tracking how the game develops for each and every shooter. Yes, this will be far more demanding then merely adhering to the previous betting strategies. While the Three Bet Plans, and the Four Bet Plan, and even the FBPD, can each be easily accommodated simply by adherence to these strategies, with the appropriate bankroll and patience, the Six Bet Plan and the other higher-risk derivatives require more abilities from you, and more dedication. With these plans and strategies, you are no longer simply making the required wagers, and then sitting back and seeing the results. Although with all of these strategies and plans you can always control your game, such control and wagering differentials become far more profound, and far more important, in these more "aggressive" strategies. Here's how the Six Bet Plan works:

Continuing with the established example of the $5 minimum bet, you begin the Six Bet Plan as with all the other front line plans shown above. Make a $5 pass line bet, and after the point has been established, back that with double odds. Then place the 6, 8, 5, and/or 9, leaving out whichever may be the point. Then buy the 4 and the 10 for at least $25, paying a 5 percent commission (in this case only the $1 because casinos will not accept the $1.25 true commission). If you can, buy the 4 and the 10 for $35, and if the casino automatically accepts only the $1 commission, keep silent and stay with this. If the casino (the dealer, probably) wants to charge you the $2 commission, explain to him (them) that under gaming regulations they cannot "overcharge" you, and that since the true commission is only $1.75, they would be defrauding you by charging the extra 25 cents— unless, that is, they wish to change the table, table signs, table limits, and table layout to fractional payoffs and commissions. Hopefully, you won't have this much trouble, since most casinos would rather accept the short commission than cause a delay in the game, a commotion, and, possibly, an angry customer likely to call the law down on them. Therefore, let us here assume for the purpose of this extended example, that you are able to buy the 4 and the 10 for $35, and pay only the $1 commission on each. Now, leaving out whatever number may be the point, your betting strategy here would play out as follows:

We will assume that the point is 5. So, now you have your original $5 pass line bet, plus $10 in free odds. You have placed the 6 and the 8 for $12 each. You have placed the 9 for $10. You have bought the 4 and the 10 for $35 each. This means you have a total of $119 exposed on the table, a total of six bets. With this plan, the benefit is immediate. You win on any roll, other than any 7, 2, 3, 12, or 11. You don't care about the 2, 3, 12, or 11. They don't affect you. The only number that can kill you on this plan is the roll of any 7 immediately after you have made this bet, or the roll of any 7 before any of the box numbers are rolled. These are the only two instances where you can lose the entire spread, without ever having hit a winner. In total, you have five chances to roll a 6 and 8 (10 total), plus four chances to roll the 5 and 9 (eight total; remember that the 5 is the point, so you will win if it is rolled and won't lose the rest of the spread, at which time you should call your bets off for the come out roll), plus three ways to roll a 4 and 10 (six total). So, in total, you have 10 + 8 + 6 = 24 chances out of 36 to hit a winner (statistically speaking). Conversely, you have six ways to roll any 7, for a loser. The 2, 3, 12, or 11 don't factor, and are neutral to this strategy (like the 7, 8, and 9 in Blackjack card counting). The 2, 3, 12, and 11 together give you a total of six ways to roll a *non-event,* as far as this strategy is concerned. Therefore, you have a total of 24 winning possibilities, a total of 6 losing possibilities, and a total of 6 neutral rolls that don't affect you at all. This means that out of 36 statistically perfect rolls, you should expect 24 winners, 6 losers, and 6 non-events, for a total of 24 winners over 6 losers (we don't count the non-event six rolls of the 2, 3, 12, or 11).

Putting this into money, you will win on at least one of the box numbers (including the point roll) 24 times over the statistically perfect 36 rolls, and lose only 6 times. Over your six bets, with a total of $119 spread, your average per-number bet is $19.83, which we will call $20 for ease of calculation and understanding. Therefore, based on this statistical formula, with this strategy you can expect to win the average $20 over 24 events, for a total statistically theoretical win of $480. Your losses are a little different. If any 7 is rolled immediately after you have made the spread group bet, then you lose the entire $119 and never have a chance to hit a winner. However, the possibility of this happening is only minor, because your overall expected loss is only six in 24 (remember, the neutral rolls don't factor). Also, if the first series of rolls are the 2, 3, 12, and/or 11, then these are the neutral rolls, and although you don't win, you also don't lose. If these rolls are then followed by any 7, then you lose the entire $119 spread, without ever having hit a winner. However, this also happens only six times out of the statistically perfect 36 rolls. Most of the time, when any 7 is rolled for your loss of the entire $119 spread, this will not happen immediately after you make the spread bet, or after several neutral rolls, followed by the any 7. Most of the time the loss of your total spread will happen after at least one of your box numbers was rolled at least once.

If your 6 and 8 are hit just once, followed by a total loss, you have made a 7:6 on your $12. If the 9 is hit (remember, in this example the 5 is the point), then you get 7:5 on your $10. If either the 4 or the 10 is rolled at least once, now you get the true odds of 2:1 on the bet, because you bought your 4 and 10 for $35 each. So, each such hit on the "buy" bets gets you a $70 profit, plus your bet of $35 stays. Just one such hit on either of these "buy" numbers will immediately reduce your overall risk exposure from $119 to only $49, since you took your $70 win. Similarly so for the other box numbers, which you can calculate for yourself. Any such single hit, before that dreaded any 7, will reduce your overall total financial exposure by that one win amount. Since at least one such win will happen at least 24 times, statistically speaking, out of the possible 36, you have a 24 in 36 chance of making at least that one winner. Why is this important? Because the *frequency of this occurrence will allow you to reduce your overall financial risk exposure, while at the same time maximizing your exposure to cumulative wins.* This is the principal and primary formula that is used to extract profits from even a negative expectation game like Craps.

You are using the diminished risk capacity model to spread your risk over a series of events, any one of which will reduce your general financial exposure to losses. At the same time, you are using the maximum yield model to extract profits from those statistical anomalies that are the swings to the contrary standard statistical norm. In plain words, this means that you will be losing less, overall, while winning several times more than your proportional relative losses. In numbers, for each diminished total loss, instead of the total $119, it will be only $49, or slightly more, depending on the win rolled, in only one instance of a win, immediately followed by the total loss of the betting spread. So, while you will suffer such a total spread loss an average of eight times (two times immediately after the come out, or after neutral rolls, plus six standard loss possibilities after one win), you will win at least one event 24 times. Diminishing your risk exposure by such single-win events will stretch your bankroll, allowing for additional events. This is important because the profitability of this strategy depends on your ability to financially withstand these sequence losses of the spread, while being in action awaiting the inevitable occurrence of several point rolls and box number rolls. Once you get past the single event win, followed by the total spread loss, you are in the positive. All this will take is the roll of at least two of your box numbers, for an average roll of 2.5 numbers, to make you an overall profit. Remember that your free odds are paid at true odds, facing no house edge; therefore your wins each time the point is rolled are greater than each time the box numbers are rolled, other than the "buy" numbers. Also remember that each time the 4 and the 10 are rolled, which are your "buy" numbers, you have maximized your bet while limiting the house edge to about 2.8 percent and "shaved" their commission to the mere $1 on each bet, while all your wins are paid off also at true odds. (The $2 total buy bet commission is not factored into the overall betting spread because this expense is more than compensated for by the act of diminishing the house edge on the buy bets, shaving the house commission, and the fact that the buy bets and the free odds on the pass line bets are paid at true odds. Consequently, the $2 total would not be correctly factored as a cost, and if so done would have required a much more complex analysis of this strategy; simply, just allow for the $2 commission on the buy bets, and lay it off on the benefits against the wins gained.)

Cumulatively considering all your bets in this Six Bet Plan as one group, what you have in effect accomplished is to force the house to give you the best bets possible and pay you off at true odds on three of the six total bets. You have gained a near statistical median of 24 in 36 possibilities of a win, diminished your risk by expectation of at least one hit before a total loss of the spread, and maximized your win potential by having all the box numbers covered with the best bets and odds available. Now, all you have to do is gain an average 2.5 hits per roll from any shooter, and if this is achieved as a *statistical average,* then you will always gain financial profits from Craps, even though this is a negative-expectation game.

This is the best method of extracting powerful profits from Craps, without the reliance on any specific system. Plainly and simply, this is a strategy based on your understanding of the game, and its bets and odds, and your ability to maximize your win potential while minimizing the house edge and your loss exposure. As you play Craps, you will quickly discover that there will be numerous times where the shooters will roll more than 2.5 of your numbers. There will be times when the numbers are rolled, then the point is made, and then the numbers are rolled again, before the final crap out, and so on. In these situations, you will gain the most money in the shortest possible time, while at the times when the rolls are cold, you will lose less. It's a very effective strategy to employ any time you are able to get the house to accept the buy bets as stated.

If you cannot get the house to accept the buy bets at $35 with only the $1 commission, then make $30 bets and try for the $1 commission. If you can't get them to agree, then do the $25 buy bet; this they will accept, because every casino I have ever visited has always accepted this. Regardless, simply adapt your financial exposure to whatever these wagering amounts may be. Now, there are only two other things for you to consider.

First, if the point is made, is what to do with all your place and buy bets on the come out roll. Some strategists suggest that it is best to leave them working, even on the come out roll. I disagree. In this Six Bet Plan, your success depends on the numbers being rolled before any 7, and not have your bets at risk needlessly on the come out roll. Without getting involved in further explanations, much of which we have already covered earlier, any time the point is made, take your wins and immediately call all your place and buy bets "off" or "down" for the next come out roll. In this strategy, you must view each come out roll as the beginning of the next session, and each crap out as the end of that session. This will help you not to overbet your bankroll, the shooter, or the table. Each time you win on the point, start everything over again. Each time you lose on a crap out, start over again. Each such event is an independent series, as far as you are concerned. Never deviate from this, or you will waste this plan, and the strategy will be compromised to a point where it will no longer be effective.

Second is what to do if the shooter, the dice, and/or the table are just not passing. Well, if this is the case, and your total spread suffered more than three consecutive total losses of the entire spread, without ever having had any winners, then you may want to change your strategy to the dark side bets. If this happens, your decisions will govern the adaptability of the remainder of your wagering strategy. Of course, you can also simply leave this table, and go else-where. This is, actually, the preferred manner: go some-where else. Continue your session series. You are the owner of the session series, not the table. Your session series goes everywhere you go. So why stay where your strategy isn't working? Well, you may want to because you want to wait until the tide turns. Often, such negative rolls (relative to your front line play) are easily followed by a like series of hot rolls. So, depending on your skills, you may wish to stop this strategy, and go with a dark side alternative. How you do this depends on you. I will show you a dark side strategy later; however, I still advise you to simply stop your play. You can stand there, and wait a few rolls. Or leave. Come back later. Go somewhere else. Stopping your series is always your best option to last out negative rolls, when playing any of these front line strategies. Simply get back in the game when you have determined, through your skills and observational analysis, that the short-term nega-tive trend has ebbed. This will enhance your strategy play for any of these front line methods, and not just this Six Bet Plan, although here it is more important because of the total cumulative risk to your bankroll on each and every roll. However, this strategy is designed to last out even these negative anomalies. Remember that you are wagering a total spread, and that no single event matters. By using the infor-mation shown here earlier, you will soon find out that even such short-term negative trends are more than compensated for by the recurrence of your wins. Since you have many more ways to win in this plan than you can lose, the choice should be obvious—stay and wait it out. This will be deter-mined by your bankroll.

To play this strategy you should have at least a $2,000 bankroll, preferably a $3,000 bankroll. This will allow you to outlast even the negative trends. Only a very short positive trend, where the shooter rolls numbers and points, will be enough to not only overcome any of your accumulated losses, but put you firmly into profit. This strategy will simply work out this way, because that's what it is designed to do. The only time you will lose is if you leave before the events complete themselves. This can happen only if you don't have enough of a bankroll at the start. If you don't have this bankroll, don't play this strategy. Play instead the more conservative Three Bet Plans. Then, work your way up. *Don't push yourself beyond your ability to sustain the inevitable losses.* If you can't handle this, don't play this strategy. It's that easy. If you do have this bankroll, then have the guts to last it out. It will turn, and you will recover. Even if you lose that session, the diminished risk capacity model incorporated into this strategy will always guarantee that your losses will be the smallest possible. Your next session can easily recover this, and then some. Remember that it is all cumulative. Nothing in any of these strategies is a single event. While the rolls of the dice are all single events, your wagering strategy is not. This is a protracted series of events, designed to accumulate end-of-session *sequence* profits. This will be so, as long as you can adhere to the principles of this Six Bet Plan, and play it to the fullest.

DARK SIDE STRATEGY

As I have stated repeatedly, the dark side bets should not be used in any part of your playing strategy, other than as a temporary divestification or deviation from your front line betting plans. Even then it's inadvisable. However, in the spirit of trying to cover everything, there may be a method to this madness after all. Well, maybe.

The best strategy is to simply reverse the first of my Three Bet Plans. Since the dark side works in the opposite manner to the front line, reversing that strategy will be the best course of action. First, make the $5 don't pass bet. Then, after the point has been established, lay the appropriate odds backing up your don't pass bet. Now, make two don't come bets. Then, hope for the crap out. That's it. Other than this, the only other possibility is to temporarily shift some of your action to the don't pass line, and directly lay against the number, making no more than two such lay bets, and only against the 4 and the 10. This will give you the best and easiest dark side strategy there can be. Now that we have satisfied even the darksiders among us, let us say no more about it.

OTHER STRATEGY OPTIONS

What I have just outlined above—the Three Bet Plans, the Four Bet Plan, the Six Bet Plan, and the short dark side strategies—is all you will actually need to make powerful profits from Craps, if you choose to play in accordance with what is traditionally explained as the "statistical model of the game of Craps." In the next chapter, "The Big Secret," I will show you that a playing strategy can also successfully include many of the "ugly" bets. While these are considered "ugly" under the statistical norm of understanding the game of Craps, my own discoveries in strategy play lead me to believe otherwise. First, however, I would like to briefly explore a few other pieces of advice that some Craps players and experts sometimes suggest.

Proposition Bets

While these are mostly in the "ugly" bets category, sometimes they may be a viable candidate, especially when incorporated into any of the above strategies. For example, you may have noticed a trend to pairs, and consequently, when playing the Six Bet Plan, you may have decided to venture a few wagers on the center propositions, the Hardways. Or, perhaps on some of the other propositions. However, such play should only be incremental, and only advisable under the most stringent of conditions, when your bankroll and your skills both allow you to make such a very risky addition to any of the above strategies. Other than that, stay away from the propositions, when considering Craps within the traditional statistical model.

Field Bets

Although not in the center layout, these are also one roll proposition bets. As discussed earlier, while the field numbers look inviting, and offer 16 chances for a winner, the truth is that they face 20 chances of a loser. That's why the house edge on the field is around 5.6 percent, or a little less around 2.8 percent if the house pays 3:1 on the 2 or the 12. The same advice applies here as for the proposition bets. Based on your skills and observation of trends, it may be a viable candidate for bets, particularly when playing the Six Bet Plan, where the field numbers 2, 3, 12, and 11 are the neutral bets. So, if you are that skilled, you can feasibly add some bets on the field to your overall Six Bet Plan, and therefore only face a loser if any 7 is rolled. This is the only viable time when field bets can be successfully employed in a Craps wagering and playing strategy.

Working on Come Out

If you have come bets, as opposed to place and buy bets, some experts suggest that it is better to have your come bets and odds working on the come out roll. If any 7 is rolled, your come bets lose, but the odds are returned to you. If a point is rolled, your come bets simply continue to work as before. If the newly rolled point is one of your come bet numbers, then your bet wins, you get the money, and that number then becomes the new point. Thereafter, everything plays as before. I agree that when you have come bets, it is always better to leave them in action at all times, and on the come out roll as well. To do this, simply ignore the dealer when he calls, "Come bets working unless called off," which is usually said after the point has been rolled. Of course, if the previous point was not rolled, then this can only mean that the shooter failed, in which case all your bets are lost. So, this argument of what to do with your come bets on the come out roll applies only to situations where the previous point was rolled, which also means that your pass line bet plus odds also won. In these cases, and only with your come bets, whichever of the plans you are playing, always have your come bets working on the come out roll, following the previously successful point pass.

However, when you are making place and buy bets, as in the other plans I have shown above, you should never have your bets working on the come out roll. Always call them off, or take them down. The reasons have already been explained, but briefly, these bets all lose if any 7 is rolled. Place and buy bets don't have free odds, and therefore the entire wager loses on the come out roll, and they are decidedly an underdog in those situations.

To keep this clear in your mind, simply remember that come bets with odds *do* work on the come out roll. Place and buy bets do *not* work on the come out roll. If you remember this, you will never make the mistake of letting place and buy bets work when they should be off, or, preferably, down.

Press and Push

This is the fun part of any strategy. This is the portion of your skills in Craps that allows you to make more money with only the original bet at risk. Pressing your bets can be done on any wager, other than the original pass line, don't pass, come, and don't come bets. Everything else can be pressed. "Pressing" your bets simply means to increase the amount of money on that bet, and is usually done after a win. Mostly, this is advantageous to place players, although come players often do this as well, by increasing the amount of the next come bet, or pressing if they are "off and on," in the event they already have all the available numbers covered with come bets (which is inadvisable, because placing and buying is a better strategy; see above).

Mostly, pressing your bets becomes a good idea only under two conditions. First, on place bets of 6 and 8, and only on those two numbers. The reasons should, by now, be obvious to you. Second, on the Hardways propositions, if you have mastered the game sufficiently so that you have been able to spot the trends and added these center propositions to your Six Bet Plan. Since these bets are not one-roll bets, but work until rolled easy, hard, or a 7-out, you can "ride the Hardways" for quite a while at minimal cost. You can start with the table minimum, and usually even $5 table minimums will allow a $1 bet on the Hardways. Then, if you hit, you can spread the win over the rest of the Hardways, and now increase your wins 2x, 3x, or more times the amount, with only your original bets at risk. This is also what is often called "pushing the house," because here you have chosen to view the series of Hardways bets as a part of your "aggressive" strategy portfolio, while risking merely the minimum at the beginning, and then adding extra money to each wager as the game continues, and as you win on these bets. That way you will always be betting more when you are winning, and betting less when you are not, while risking only the minimum at all times.

For the sake of an easy example, let's assume that you have made Hardways bets for $1 on each of the four Hardways propositions. In addition, hopefully, to your other playing strategy, you have added the $4 total risk to the "aggressive" portion of your strategy playing portfolio. Now, if you hit on, say, the hard 6, you get paid 9:1, often shown as 10 for 1 (or you should get it, and if you are playing on a table where the pay is only 9 for 1 then you haven't been paying attention to what has been written in this book, or any other for that matter). This means you now have $9 more, plus the remaining $4 on the Hardways spread. Now, you can take $4 from that $9 profit, and press your Hardways by $1 each, still leaving you with $5 in overall profit, over that spread. So, now you have covered not only your original $4 investment, but have been able to press your bets to $2 on each of the Hardways, and still pocket $5. Now, all the $8 riding on the Hardways is *house money*! None of your own money is now at risk. So, if you hit another Hardways bet, say the 8, now you get the 9:1 on the $2 bet—and this bet, as well as all the other bets, is not your original money! All of this is now extra found money. You now get $18 for your $2 bet, and still have the $8 left on the layout. You can repeat the procedure, and keep pressing each time you win. Whenever any one of the Hardways numbers is rolled easy, take all the bets down, pocket your profits, and start over again on the next roll with the minimum $1 bet (or whatever the amount of money that you will determine will be your minimum bet, as determined by your bankroll and your personal financial situation).

This is the best way to make powerful profits from Craps fast, and with the least risk. However, doing this by only betting the propositions is a prescription for disaster, unless you are playing something like my Big Secret, but that's a different matter entirely. Playing Craps in accordance with the traditional model, and only betting the propositions, will lead to your overall financial ruin. Always, and all the time. It simply doesn't matter what you do. If you play these propositions only, and only this way, without the added cover of the previously shown strategies, then no matter how many times you can press your bet, eventually the losses will overcome you. So, it is very important that you remember never to press your place bets, or your proposition bets, unless you are first in a positive result period of your primary strategy. Only then does it become advisable to add these bets, and these presses, to your overall playing strategy, and only temporarily, based on your skills in being able to determine the rolls as they happen to be doing at that particular table, at that particular moment. That's why even though Craps is a game based on independent events whose outcome doesn't seem to require any skills, such a perception is hugely in error. Craps requires a great deal of skill. However, these skills have nothing to do with the ability to roll the dice. These skills have everything to do with your ability to exploit the game based on your abilities to observe, adapt, and always play in accordance with one of the strategies I have shown. That way, you will face the least risk, with the highest expected profits.

8

The Big Secret

What follows in this short chapter is my own strategy for exploiting a certain aspect of Craps often ignored by other strategists. Most people would consider this a "system," but I do not like the negative connotations of the word "system," since it often means something "flaky" or something that can be called a "con." I prefer to refer to my strategy as a "method," because I have developed this not as some "sure-fire system" but rather as a dedicated approach to this game, requiring knowledge, bankroll, patience, persistence, ability, skills, discipline, and game management. Applied properly, this method of play preserves wins in the majority of instances, for an overall profitability at end-of-sessions. For an example of the session block method (used as the basis for this Craps playing method), please refer to my book *Powerful Profits from Blackjack.* In that book I outline a 10-event, 10-session principle of play that is adaptable to this Craps method. In fact, it should be learned first, and then this Craps method applied to it.

Before proceeding, however, it is very important that

you understand that the Craps playing method I am here presenting is founded completely on an approach entirely contrary to the overall accepted norm of understanding the game from within the mathematical statistical model. The bets I propose are all among the "ugly" bets, those that face the highest house edge, and are therefore universally shown, in books and writings about Craps, as the bets to avoid. Even I have so stated, and for a good reason.

There are two ways to approach playing Craps. The first is to understand the game from within that traditionally understood mathematical statistical model, and therefore adhere to the principles of frequency occurrence, and thus their derived percentages and odds. The second way to play Craps is to completely discount these traditional theories and treat Craps as a game of chaotic events in no particular order, without any foundation in anything empirical. Applying this theory of chaos to Craps is to fly directly in the face of all established science. Since all science and mathematics flounder in their inability to account for the reality of a chaotic universe, and indeed discount the application of the theory of chaos to any scientific endeavor, the proponents of any methods in compliance with these empirically derived assumptions jointly ignore that their own perspectives are simply grounded in an unvalidated assumption—that of an ordered universe that can be understood through reason and rational analysis. That is plainly not so, but is a position which no scientist will allow himself to accept, because that would destroy the very foundation upon which such thinking allows us to function as a species, and as masters of the material entities. While such thinking can easily allow us to make things, like TVs, cars, rockets, hot dogs, Slurpees, and so on, it all hinges on each future event having some kind of a rational relation to past occurrences. Hence the derived theories of event-relativity and objective statistics.

Although I understand these needs, and as a member of this human species I also work within such models to allow anything to be communicated to others, there are times when I seek to enlighten the general readership and point out the inherent folly and flaw of such structured thinking, especially as it applies to the overreliance on mathematics and their derivative formulae. In particular, I often choose to apply this model to gambling games, because by far and large these have been so over-mathematized that the understanding of these games has reached the level of dogma. "Always do this, never do that" are expressions seen in just about every book on any casino game. All of this is based on that erroneous formulaic understanding of the flawed assumptive reasoning that has so infected the thinking of mankind for centuries. While I use these models as part of my workability principle, because they are highly useful as tools for explanation, I also like to deviate somewhat from this traditional thinking and try to show that even those "ugly" events can yield a financial profit. And therein lies the most basic difference between my approach and that of the vast majority of other gaming writers, authors, and experts. In my view, playing Craps is not an exercise to validate the mathematical statistical model. Instead, playing Craps is for the purpose of financial profit. To make money. That's it. And so on for the other casino games about which I write in my books.

This failure to differentiate between the drive to validate the statistics and the objective of making money from the game is what limits most books on Craps, and indeed on all the other casino games. These limitations are vested in the flawed assumptive understanding of event-relativity. While many strategies of play can exploit even that flawed model of rationalist convention, such as those strategies I have listed in my Three Bet Plans, the Four Bet Plan, and the Six Bet Plan, and their derived adaptability to additional wagers, the possibility also exists to develop a wagering method that doesn't rely on these conventions. This, therefore, is what you will find here. I call this my Craps Strategy Two. The reason is because there are more than one, and this one happens to be the second.

Let us explore the possibility of making money by using the worst bets in Craps, and doing so with little or no risk to our bankroll over all applied sessions. In fact, if played correctly, this method never loses. Yes, of course there will be losses, and losing events, and even losing sessions. But, over the number of applied sessions these will be more than compensated for by the overall approach to these events. Grouped as a whole, all sessions combined allow for an overall 60 percent loss rate in events, while resulting in a positive cash excess. Simply put, playing this correctly will, over the applied sessions, yield a positive financial result even if you suffer 60 percent losses in individual events. Put another way, you can win only 40 percent of the time, and still make money. Sounds strange? It sure is. It is the X-treme Craps, and I guess that's the best way to put it in the current colloquialisms of the day. If you still doubt, look ahead at the sample events in Chart One and Chart Two. Do remember, however, that what you are looking at is only one session from a group of applied sessions; and while this clearly shows the profitability even in the face of adversity, the total picture can only be viewed when you apply this to protracted series of events. Your own play will provide the proof and validation. I make no excuses for it, and no claims. All I'm saying is that I have found this to be workable, profitable, and achievable. You decide if this is so, or not.

CRAPS STRATEGY TWO—HARDWAYS

This strategy is based on the following principles:

A. Starting bet of $5 on the pass line, NO ODDS.
B. Starting bet of $5 on EACH of the four Hardways: 4, 6, 8, and 10.
C. Incremental increases on the Hardways by $1 each time a LOSS occurs on ANY ONE, or such an increase on ALL if a total loss occurs (which can happen only on crap out).

Rules

- Always make a $5 starting bet on the pass line, NO ODDS, on the come out roll.
- After the point is established, make $5 bets on ALL the Hardways.
- From then on, each time ANY Hardways bet LOSES, press *that bet* by $1 for the next sequence, and so on.
- If ALL the Hardways bets lose (on seven-out), PRESS ALL Hardways bets by $1 next time the NEW point is established. For example, if the bets on the 4 and the 6 were at $6 each, and the 10 was at $9, and the 8 was at $5, press them ALL by $1 next time, so that now you have $7 each on the 4 and the 6, and $10 on the 10, and $6 on the 8. And so on. This can get tricky, but that's where your mental skills come into play. You can help yourself do this by using the rail to prepare your next sequence of bets for all the bets, using single chips as dividers for your next-bet amounts.
- Each time ANY Hardways bet WINS, take the win and let the bet ride at the previous bet level.

- ONLY INCREASE YOUR BETS AFTER A LOSS, and ONLY on that *one* number that lost, OR on *all* numbers *on crap out.*

Keys to Remember

(i) Any sequence begins with a come out roll, and ends with a crap out.
(ii) If the point IS made, the sequence continues because Hardways do NOT automatically lose in this case; they should be simply called OFF for the next come out roll, and then called WORKING again after the point has been established, for the continuation of that sequence roll.

Bankroll

Minimum $1,000. Recommend $2,500. If you wish to play at higher levels, simply prorate the base $5 unit to whatever the amount you wish to establish as your minimum betting unit, and then work the method by incremental increases relative to that amount.

Test Case Analysis

The charts on pages 199 and 200 represent one of the thousands of test cases that were incorporated into the process of creating this strategy.

Each ROLL is identified by a letter, and ALL the sequences here shown constitute ONE test and session. Each lettered roll is a come out roll, followed by the results. Each sequence ends with a crap out. If the point *is* made, the sequence continues. Each entire session can ONLY END with a crap out.

The asterisk (*) signifies the POINT.

The letter (e) AFTER any Hardways number signifies that this number was rolled EASY, meaning a loss of that Hardways bet, signifying that an incremental increase was called for.

The letter (h) AFTER any Hardways number signifies that this number was rolled the HARD WAY, meaning that a WIN was made and that the bet now remains at the previous bet level, until the next event calls for its increase.

COMMENTARY

The first thing that will strike anyone who has knowledge of gambling systems is that this is a version of the Incremental Martingale. The Standard Martingale calls for the bets to be doubled after each loss. The Super Martingale calls for each bet to be tripled, or quadrupled, after each loss. No matter how you view any of these systems, the plain truth is that all of the systems of this kind rely on the *negative* progression. This means to *add more money after a loss.* Most gaming experts will agree that the only time a player should increase his bets is after a *win,* and not after a loss. Indeed, the Pressing Strategies for Craps, or for any other gambling game, rely heavily on this advice. It is very good advice, when considering the standard approach to the game. It is always advisable to increase your bets with money won, rather than the other way around; increasing after losses exposes you to the risk of losing more of your own money.

The Incremental Martingale system calls for the increase of bets after a loss, but not by double the amount. Instead, this version of the progressive betting system calls

CRAPS - STRATEGY TWO - CHART

ROLL	RESULTS OF ROLL															NOTES
A	8*	7														crap out
B	3	4*	6e	5	5	9	9	7								crap out
C	6*	8e	7													crap out
D	6*	10h	7													crap out
E	9*	11	6e	5	5	3	6h	11	10e	2	4e	8e	4e	6	9	point wins
F	7	9*	4e	4e	6e	12	2	7								crap out
G	10*	5	6h	5	4h	3	8h	4e	5	9	6h	5	7			crap out
H	8*	9	2	8e												point wins
I	7	4*	7													crap out
J	8*	8h														point wins
K	2	7	7	5*	11	3	11	9	6e	10h	11	9	6e	3		crap out
L	4*	8e	7													crap out
M	11	12	8*	7												crap out
N	4*	7														crap out
O	3	8*	9	10h	10e	8e										point wins
P	6*	9	2	9	12	6e										point wins
Q	7	9*	6e	11	8e	3	10e	10h	10e	9						point wins
R	7	8*	3	7												crap out
S	9*	5	8e	5	3	4e	5	5	4e	4h	3e	11	4h	7		crap out
T	2	10*	9	2	7											crap out
U	3	11	9*	4h	4e	9										point wins
V	7	6*	5	4e	6h	5	10h	2	6e							point wins
W	7	5*	5	2	5	10h										point wins
X	7	7	10*	5	10h											point wins
Y	6*	7														crap out
Z	5*	7														crap out
AA	7	3	7	8*	9	9	3	5	9	12	11	8e				point wins
BB	10*	7														crap out
CC	2	7	9*	8e	3e	7										crap out
DD	7	11	10*	7												crap out—here we end the test

199

ANALYSIS OF BETS

ROLL	PROGRESSION OF BETS 4	6	8	10	SEQUENCE LOSS	SEQUENCE WIN	
A	5	5	5	5	25	0	Loss of all bets on crap out
B	6	7	5	6	35	0	ditto
C	7	8	8	7	35	0	ditto
D	8	9	9	8	34	68	win on hard 10
E	11	11	11	10	0	99	win on hard 6 and win on point, therefore no loss
F	14	13	12	11	60	0	win $5 on come out 7, but loss of $5 on crap out, so no win
G	16	14	13	12	60	481	wins on hard 6, hard 4, hard 8, and hard 6 made this profit
H	17	15	14	13	0	5	pass line winner
I	18	16	15	14	68	0	pass line win but then crap out = no win
J	18	17	16	15	0	144	the 8 was the point and it won
K	19	19	17	15	70	105	crap 2 plus two win 7's plus crap out = wash - no win on pass line bet
L	20	20	19	18	80	0	
M	21	21	20	17	84	0	FROM NOW ON THE REST OF THE ANALYSIS SHOULD BE OBVIOUS
N	22	22	21	13	68	0	
O	23	23	23	20	0	140	
P	24	26	24	21	0	5	
Q	25	28	26	24	0	168	
R	26	29	27	25	107	0	
S	29	30	30	26	120	406	
T	30	31	31	27	128	0	
U	31	32	32	28	0	217	
V	32	32	32	29	0	481	
W	32	32	32	29	0	5	
X	32	32	32	29	0	218	Hard 10 was the point, line wins, plus two 7's wins on come out
Y	32	32	32	29	130	0	
Z	33	33	33	30	134	0	
AA	34	34	34	30	0	5	
BB	34	34	35	30	138	0	
CC	35	35	37	31	143	0	
DD	38	36	38	32	142	5	Here we end sequences and test session

TOTAL LOSS FOR ENTIRE SESSION	$1,672	
TOTAL WIN FOR ENTIRE SESSION	$2,550	
FINAL RESULT = PROFIT OF	$878	

NOTE: We had 19 losing events and 16 winning events, meaning more losing events than winning ones, yet we still made an overall profit in the end. That is the point of this method. Each sequence is an independent event unto itself. At the end of the string of sequences—the sequence block—add up wins and subtract the losses. This gives you the final net profit.

for an increase only in *increments*. This means a fractional increase, based on the expectation of a certain sequence of events whereby it is not necessary to double, or triple, or quadruple, the next bet, and still obtain an eventual win. As with all versions of the Martingale, the problem is always twofold. First, the staggering amounts that would sometimes be necessary to wager merely to win the amount of the original bet. For example, as I have shown in my book *Powerful Profits from Blackjack,* a player could easily be forced by this system to wager over $40,000 merely to win the $5 original bet. This is ludicrous. Second, most of the time any player of such a system would easily and quickly run up against the house limits, thereby defeating the purpose. It is the second of these, the house table limits, that prevent the Martingale, and all of its standard derivatives, from being a viable candidate as a seriously useful gambling system. If it weren't for table limits, then the Martingale would always work. Eventually, the player would win. Even if the protracted series of losing events were to be over a billion dollars' worth of wagers, the simple fact of event occurrence will always provide that one winning event that recoups the player his money, and provides that initial starting bet amount profit. Although these sums could be staggering, this system would always produce a winner, eventually. Since no casino will allow this to happen, and since most people do not have such infinite funds to risk, this system is not only not workable, but basically bogus.

With an Incremental Martingale, however, we are now starting to see a difference. Instead of calling for the bets to be doubled or otherwise increased depending on which version of this system you happen to be playing (or trying to play, theoretically), now the increases after each loss are only a *fraction* of the original bet. The effect of this is to extend the protracted series of events, and allow for an increased streak to occur before hitting the house limits.

Although theoretically feasible, the problem is that the traditional Martingale approach simply cannot work in increments. Unless, that is, you apply this to events that pay off at odds. You see, the traditional Martingale system was developed for events that pay off at even money. The Incremental Martingale was later developed to work for games such as Roulette, where the single number payoffs are 35:1 and, therefore, you can start with $1, then go to $2, then to $3, then to $4, then to $5, and so on, in increments that are not double the size of your previous bet, as is the case with the traditional Martingale. This still assures you of a win, when the number hits. The problem is that the number won't always hit within the statistical norm of once in 38 spins. It can *not hit* for very long periods of time, and this will defeat the purpose of that application of the Martingale to those odds events.

What I have done, in this version of my Craps method, is to use the principle of the Incremental Martingale with the principles of tiered wagering and fractional differential within the confines of the Group Wagering Strategy.

I have used the core of the odds pay Hardways, on tables paying 9:1 and 7:1 (or those where these payoffs are listed as 10 for 1 and 8 for 1, which is the same thing), and divided them into individual increments, while at the same time keeping them together as a group. It will take a little mental gymnastics to grasp this, but it is very simple. Since we start with a $5 bet on each of the Hardways, which is traditionally higher than most table minimums of $1 on each bet, we begin the series with a total capital risk of $25—$5 on the front line, no odds, and $5 each on the four Hardways. The only reason why the $5 front line bet is there is because it wins when a 7 or an 11 is rolled on the come out roll. This provides a small hedge for several of the line losses on crap out. The reason why there are no odds is because they are not necessary for this method, and their expenditure, when lost, is too much to be recouped by this method of play. Actually, the front line bet does not have to be there for this method to work; however, I advise you to do it exactly as stated, because those few times the front line bets win will add those precious extra values to your *overall* bottom line. It will also help to hide the fact that you are playing a system, and that's the most important reason to make the bet.

The core of this method are the four Hardways. We start with the $5 bet on each, but each time one loses, we press it only incrementally, by $1. That's why we will often wind up with four bets, each at a different level. For this reason, to keep accurate track of these increments, it is also necessary to forego any other bets. Keeping these bets straight is all that is required, other than the one front line wager. By increasing each one after it loses by that $1 amount, we grow each Hardways without the necessity of growing the others in negative situations. Each time any hardway *wins,* we *take the profit* and let that bet ride at its previous levels, and do *not* increase it, or any of the others. After crap out, when we lose all Hardways bets, we start the next series with the incremental increase of $1 added to *all* the Hardways. This way, *we always grow the bets.* (The only exception to growing the bets is the front line bet, which we always leave the same, since it doesn't factor significantly for the overall method. It is there largely to help hide the fact that we are playing a system—leaving it always the same, with no odds, makes us look like the perennial loser to the casino.)

So, as with the example above, you must have the next series of bets ready for each crap out possibility. If you don't, the dealers will scrape off the propositions and you can easily lose track of how much you had spread. This will defeat the purpose of the series. Each time there is a crap out, you will lose all your Hardways. It is at this time, and *only* at this time, when you increase *all* the Hardways by that $1 increment. In all other cases, whenever any individual hardway number loses, by being rolled easy, you press that one number only by that $1, while the remaining numbers stay at whatever wager level they happen to be. Whenever any Hardways number wins, you take that win and let the bet ride at its current level, and leave everything else alone. This will assure you always of taking the win and always growing the wager, while not risking your profits.

For those of you with larger bankrolls, simply increase the amount of the base wager, and then add the differential to each of your increases. In the case of the $5 base wager, the increases are one-fifth, in this case $1. If you are wagering a $50 base bet on each, then your increases would be one-fifth, or $10, and so on. Whatever your amount of the base wager, use the one-fifth formula to get to your incremental increases. However, be aware of the table limits, and make sure that none of your protracted series of events will hit that ceiling.

In effect what we are doing with this method is "milking the Martingale." By spreading our bets into a group of four, we widen the scope of potential wins. By increasing only the *one* losing number, we are *limiting the exposure to wager increases after a loss.* By betting on events that pay off at positive odds, we maximize the yield of profits. By playing tables with a $5 minimum and traditionally a $500 to $5,000 maximum, we will never be in danger of hitting the table ceiling on these bets—it will simply not be possible, because we will either win, or lose, much more frequently than any single series of protracted negative events can occur, as could be the case in Blackjack or Roulette. We can easily increase the value of these bets, by playing on tables with a $25 minimum and a $10,000 to $25,000 maximum. For high rollers, this application still works just as well. We will still never hit the house ceiling, and get the maximum value from these "ugly" bets in a protracted series of events, while minimizing exposure. This is a combination of the Incremental Martingale with my tiered and fractional differential wagering, combined additionally with a group bet strategy, while allowing for individual variances within the group.

If you look carefully at the charts, you will see that even this small slice of a test provides an end-result profitability, completely regardless of what actually happened on the Craps table during that series. In fact, you don't even have to be aware of what is going on at the Craps game, other than to keep track of your bets within this method. If this is further combined with the series of sessions and session blocks, you now have a method that provides a financial profit on a steady basis while betting on "ugly" house bets. What makes this possible are the methods of betting and increasing the wagers, but also the fact of the odds payoff on those events.

However, don't play this on tables where the payoffs are 9 for 1 and 7 for 1, instead of 9 to 1 and 7 to 1. If they are listed as 10 for 1 and 8 for 1, then this is okay, because that's the same as 9:1 and 7:1, as I have explained earlier (see Chapter Five for details, if you can't recall that discussion right this moment).

Although this method will still work even on the lesser payoffs on mixed tables where the pays were shaved to the "for 1" below the traditional payouts, you will be losing the base unit bet amount each time you hit a winner, and this will substantially alter your win expectations.

Finally, I know that I am bound to have a plethora of critics in regard to this method of playing Craps. I cautioned you earlier that this is a method vested in an entirely different perspective of perceived reality, and that it has nothing to do with the traditional understanding of the game of Craps. You should not allow this method to corrupt your strategy play at Craps, when applying the strategies I showed in the previous chapter. Those strategies work. They will produce more winners for you than playing Craps merely on hunches. However, if you want to be adventurous, and try your hand at something wild, then try this method. If you do it correctly, it works. Of course, I am not a guru; I cannot "see the future," and know how you will perform using this method of play. I can only suggest, and recommend, and advise. I have no problem in receiving criticism. In my tests, this works. I will leave it up to you to decide how well.

The Craps Quiz

Okay, we are now at the end of all the hard stuff. Now you can test your knowledge in this easy quiz. As the Dentist said in the film *Little Shop of Horrors,* "It's painless. Trust me!" Well, let us fill our glasses with Novocain, and let's go.

QUIZ QUESTIONS

QUESTION 1

Do the mathematics of Craps show that the game can be beaten?

ANSWER
    A. Craps is a negative expectation game, and therefore, understood within the mathematical model, it cannot be beaten.
    B. Only when playing a correct strategy.
    C. Theoretically, yes.
    D. Only if you are a dice slider.

QUESTION 2

Can Craps be beaten for financial profits?

ANSWER

A. Only if you are an expert player.
B. Only if the rules allow it.
C. Only if the pit boss lets you.
D. Only if you play correctly and use all your knowledge of the game, including proper playing strategies.

QUESTION 3

How do you identify a "good" game?

ANSWER

A. One where lots of players are yelling and screaming and having a great time.
B. One where the dice pass a lot.
C. One where there is heavy action on the dark side.
D. One where lots of players are winning.

QUESTION 4

Which of the following are the "good" rules and options?

ANSWER

A. All odds bets pay off at odds "for 1."
B. The field pays 2:1 for 2 or 12.
C. The table layout includes Big 6 and Big 8.
D. None of the above.

QUESTION 5

How can you beat Craps consistently and for profit?

ANSWER
   A. By learning to become a dice slider.
   B. By learning to become a dice mechanic and control the rolls.
   C. By becoming a "rhythmic roller."
   D. By understanding that Craps cannot be beaten, statistically, but that using the correct playing strategies the game can yield financial profits if played in accordance with these strategies and the Keys to Winning.

QUESTION 6
How can financial profits be made from playing Craps?

ANSWER
   A. By betting large sums of money on everything available.
   B. By betting the most numbers possible.
   C. By learning and adhering to the Three, Four, and/or Six Bet Plans.
   D. By doubling your bets after each loss.

QUESTION 7
Which of the following represents the worst game?

ANSWER
   A. A table layout touting the Big 6 and Big 8.
   B. A game paying off at odds "for 1."
   C. A table where you can't buy the 4 and the 10 for at least $25 while paying only a $1 commission.
   D. All of the above.

QUESTION 8

A Craps game where the dice move around the table from player to player frequently is better, because:

ANSWER
   A. It helps to prevent cheating.
   B. It helps to speed up the game, giving you more rolls and therefore more winners.
   C. It's actually bad, because this means the dice aren't passing and therefore players on the front line are losing.
   D. It helps to get the dice to you faster.

QUESTION 9

When the dice are moving from player to player around the table frequently, you should:

ANSWER
   A. Be glad because you will get to roll the dice sooner.
   B. Beware, because frontliners are losing, and so you should consider moving your bets temporarily to the dark side.
   C. Wait for the dice to come to you, and then ask for new dice.
   D. When it's your turn, take the dice and throw them off the table, and then ask for new dice so that the cold dice won't be back in the game again.

QUESTION 10

Can casinos cheat at the game of Craps?

ANSWER
   A. Yes, they can, but would never allow this to happen because that would risk their license.

B. Yes, they can, but would never try it against the regular players who only bet small.
C. No, they can't, because they are watched by cameras all the time.
D. Yes, they can, but not very often because big players would get wise and stop playing.

QUESTION 11
You should tip the dealers well, because:

ANSWER
A. When you tip they will give you the hot dice.
B. You realize that dealers work for minimum wage and rely on tips for their income.
C. Dealers need the tip money to replace the money they lose to the customers.
D. When you tip, the dealer will sometimes pay you even on losing rolls.

QUESTION 12
You should always "hedge" your bet, because:

ANSWER
A. You will save yourself a lot of money by covering the losing bets, especially on the come out roll.
B. A "hedge" bet is simply a very good bet.
C. It is not a good bet because it will cost you more by exposing you to a higher house edge; in effect, you are hedging a good low-house-edge bet by making a bad high-house-edge bet.
D. If a shooter has been rolling for a while, the chances are he will crap out and, therefore, hedging your bets is always a good idea.

QUESTION 13
You can win big in Craps, because:

ANSWER
A. When you bet big, you win big.
B. By applying your knowledge and skill your wins will accumulate.
C. Gamblers who bet big are always welcome.
D. Players who make big bets are the only ones allowed to win big.

QUESTION 14
You should bet the dark side, because:

ANSWER
A. The casinos change dice at 3:00 A.M., and therefore the dice are always cold at that time, and the dark side wins more often.
B. Only infrequently, based on observation of the game, and then only on a few bets.
C. Always, because these bets are the favorite to win, statistically speaking.
D. It's not the best way to win, but is one of the better ways available, although not perfect.

QUESTION 15
Every Craps player should learn a playing strategy, because:

ANSWER
A. Without knowing at least one, the player can at best only hope for a win and has no idea what to do, or what to do correctly, to maximize the win.

B. It provides a framework upon which to build Craps playing skills.
C. It lets you formalize various decisions so that you always know what to do.
D. All of the above.

QUESTION 16
The Craps Strategy Two, created by this author, is successful because:

ANSWER
A. He says so.
B. It is just as good as any strategy for Craps.
C. It helps to put everything together at the same time.
D. It is still largely a suggestion, because its practical and theoretical test samples have only yielded several thousand events, while the complete proof will require several million events, although the author is pretty certain that the eventual events will prove out the premise.

QUESTION 17
When it's your turn to roll the dice and you immediately roll craps, and then crap out, you should forthwith:

ANSWER
A. Run for cover, then yell for help.
B. Immediately visit your pastor, priest, or rabbi and beg forgiveness.
C. Realize that this may happen, and perhaps bet the dark side against yourself.
D. Start crying and beg the dealer for half your money back.

QUESTION 18

You should always bet the field, because:

ANSWER

A. You have 16 ways to win.
B. It's the best of the propositions.
C. The 2 and the 12 sometimes pay 3:1, and therefore this bet on these tables is best.
D. It's never a good idea, because the field wins 16 times, but loses 20 times.

QUESTION 19

You should always place all the box numbers as "all across," because:

ANSWER

A. This way you will have all the numbers covered and will win immediately.
B. You will have all the numbers covered and will win even if the number is only rolled once.
C. Placing all the numbers is better than buying or laying them.
D. An "all across" bet is a high house edge bet, and is not a good way to play.

QUESTION 20

You should always "buy" the 6 and the 8, because:

ANSWER

A. You can "push the house" and get higher wagers in play at a low house vig.
B. Buying these numbers will get you a payoff at true odds, and therefore a lower house edge.
C. The 6 and the 8 are best bet as place bets, not buy bets.
D. You should never do this unless you want to be called a Craps Bonehead.

QUIZ ANSWERS

1. The answer is A. Since Craps is a negative-expectation game, it cannot be statistically beaten. Even by using the 100x odds backing up the front line bet, and reducing the house edge to a mere 0.02 percent, this still means that the game will always "win" that two cents out of every $100 wagered for the game's owner, the casino. Although we can make *financial* profits, that was not the point of this question.

2. The answer is D. That should be obvious by now. If it isn't, you need to read the book again.

3. The answer is A. It could also be B and D. If there are lots of players yelling and screaming at a Craps table, this usually means that the dice are passing a lot and lots of players are winning. All three are viable answers helping to identify a "good" game. However, please note that here the question had more to do with the immediate identification of a good game, rather than with the investigation of the table's layout and odds. A good game needs to have players who are winning and having a good time, but also a table with better odds. Score either A, B, or D.

4. The answer is D. None of these are "good" for your game. Stay away from these tables and bets.

5. The answer is D. If that isn't obvious, you should read the book again, or maybe choose a different game, like Bingo.

6. The answer is C. The strategies that I have shown are the simplest, easiest, and least risky methods of playing Craps for profit. If you get really good at the game, then you can try more adventurous strategies, such as those for the additional Six Bet Plan covers, as well as my Big Secret. Those, however, are only for players who know the game very well. For the simplest methods, the Three Bet Plans, and the Four Bet Plan, are the best, within the standard model.

7. The answer is D. All of these are indicators of a lousy table. Go play somewhere else.

8. The answer is C. If the dice are moving from player to player, this can only mean that shooters are crapping out a lot, not making points and not rolling numbers. This is an indication of negative rolls, meaning losers for frontliners. Here you should either sit out these rolls, leave the game and go somewhere else, or, if you are that good, bet the dark side for a while, until you see a turn back toward the right way players.

9. The answer is B. If you have answered the above question correctly, then this should have been obvious. If not, well, you need to go back and study some more.

10. The answer is A. Yes, of course they can cheat. They can in all games. But they do not, and will not! Casinos make billions of dollars a year, legally. Why would any such enterprise risk losing their gaming license, and the confidence of its stockholders, to cheat you out of your few hundred or thousand dollars? It just won't happen, not in any major U.S. casino. It's simply not worth it for the casino to do this to its customers. Customers, on the other hand, often try to cheat the casinos. That's why casino surveillance systems are among the best in the world. Cheats get caught, no matter who they are. But casinos will not cheat you. It would be economically stupid to give up a billion dollars plus per year in revenue, merely in order to cheat you for your $100 bet spread.

11. The answer is B. Casino workers generally work for minimum wage. That's $5.15 per hour in 2002. In a 40-hour workweek, they earn only $206 gross. This is merely $824 per month. From this, their deductions are made—state and social security and disability taxes, insurance, retirement plans, and so on. Then the IRS takes the rest, and so these poorest of all workers wind up either without any paycheck at all, or owing money to the government, even though they

make less in one month than their elected representatives spend on lunch in one day. This is not fair, and not just to these workers. It is a travesty of American justice for all workers who labor for these unlivable wages. Therefore, tips are essential. Without them, casino workers would not be able to survive, and none would be able to work there. Tip generously. Especially when you are winning. Remember your own life—would *you* be able to live on what they make?

12. The answer is C. It should be plainly obvious. If not, refer back to the section on hedge bets.

13. The answer is B. If you've paid attention to this book, this will be easy for you to answer.

14. The answer is B. The dark side bets do have their place in Craps, but they are better used as infrequent departures from your front line strategy play, and only in circumstances where you have been paying close attention to the game and have understood a temporary trend against the numbers. Otherwise, don't even think of this, and stick to the strategies as shown. They will win even when these negative trends happen. Be patient. Better to wait out a few rolls, or leave and find another game, or come back later, than to make an error and bet the dark side when all it was was just a one- or two-roll anomaly.

15. The answer is D. If that isn't obvious, you should go bowling instead.

16. The answer is D. It is self-explanatory.

17. The answer is C. Recognize that you may not be a right way shooter. Bet against yourself, if this happens, and don't listen to the snickers from the other players. You are there to win money. So, if you are a cold shooter, recognize that, and pass the dice, or bet the dark side.

18. The answer is D. If we choose to approach Craps from the traditional perspective, then the field is never a good bet because it yields a high house edge. It can, how-

ever, be used as part of expanded strategies, such as an expanded Six Bet Plan, but this should only be done by players who know the game very, very well, and then only in certain circumstances.

19. The answer is D. The "all across" bet is not a good one, because it forces you to place high house edge place bets such as the 5 and the 9 and, particularly, the 4 and the 10. Instead, you should use the Four Bet Plan, or perhaps the Six Bet Plan.

20. The answer is C. However, an answer of D will also be scored correctly, because if you buy the 6 and the 8 you are truly a Craps Bonehead. You should *place* the 6 and the 8, not *buy* them. You *should* buy the 4 and the 10. If you didn't know this, go get your bowling shoes or Bingo daubers because those are the games for you. Or, read the book again and pay closer attention to what you are reading.

SCORING

So here we are, at the end of the Quiz. How did you do? Score +10 points for each correct answer, and -10 points for each incorrect answer.

Total score 60 or less

You need a lot of help. Try reading the book again, and make notes. You must have missed something.

Total score 70–90

Not too bad. You are close, but must have missed a lot of details at some point. I suggest you go and start the book from the top, and take some notes.

Total score 0

This is the 50/50 spot. If you scored 0, then this means you got half the questions right, and half of them wrong. Find out which ones were wrong, and why you answered them the way you did. Then go back through the book and find out why you chose those answers, and take the test again. You should do better the next time.

Total score 110–120

Pretty good! You are well on your way. But you need some extra help, so try to find out why you answered some of the questions the way you did, and learn a little more.

Total score 130–150

Very good! You are close to becoming a good player. Just keep working.

Total score 160–170

You have done very well indeed! Now find out where you answered incorrectly, and try again.

Total score 180–190

You are really, really good! I'm proud of you! Just a little more and you've got it.

Total score 200

Wow! A perfect score! You are the expert. Now go to the casino and make some money.

Postscript

In all my books I try to strike a balance between simplifying the game and making it understandable for the novice, while at the same time providing something to advance the knowledge of readers who may already know the game, and also offering something new even for the expert. This is very hard to do. I often wonder if some of my readers will be disappointed because there was too much simplification, while others may think there was too much detail, and too much emphasis on professional play. In the final tally, I try to make these casino games easy to understand and easy to play, and to offer methods and strategies that will make it possible for the novice, the intermediate, and the expert to make a profit.

Craps can be a difficult game. It is perhaps the only casino game where so many options and methods of play can all be used at the same time. That's also why this is such a great game. It is too bad that so many players avoid it, or don't play it as it can be played. In this book, it was my hope to further the cause of this game, to show you that you can play it easily, without difficulty, and without fear. If you choose casino gambling as your form of entertainment, then it should also be a worthwhile source of fun, as well as profit. Just because casino gambling is entertaining, or at least it should be, doesn't mean it has to always make you a loser. You can win, even if you are only a casual player. You can also win if you are a more serious player. Casino players win money every day. The only reason why casinos make so much more is because so many players simply play so badly. You don't have to be one of them.

That's what I hoped to accomplish in this book—to show you that way. Now, the rest is up to you. How well you do in your actual casino play will depend on how well you can apply what has been shown. That in itself isn't easy, but it can be done. Don't consider yourself a failure if you don't accomplish all your goals the very first time you try. Craps will take a while to master. Similarly, don't stay away from the game because you think it's so complex. It isn't, and it can be played by everyone, easily, and with great enjoyment. It is the enjoyment of the game with which I now leave you, and wish you all the very best.

Recommended Reading

Among the many excellent books on Craps, I wish to refer you to a few that I have found to be among the best and most informative. All these authors are my friends and associates, and I wish to thank them for their efforts. Their books have been most beneficial to me in my own understanding of the game of Craps. I heartily recommend them as part of your Craps library.

The Craps Answer Book (2001), by John Grochowski. Bonus Books, 160 East Illinois Street, Chicago, IL 60611.

Beat the Craps Out of the Casinos and *Forever Craps* (both 2000), both by Frank Scoblete. Bonus Books, 160 East Illinois Street, Chicago, IL 60611.

Craps: Take the Money and Run (1995), by Henry Tamburin. Research Services Unlimited, PO Box 19727, Greensboro, NC 27419.

I also mentioned an article by Alan Krigman, which appeared in the Las Vegas newspaper *Gaming Today*. This article was in the June 11–17, 2002, issue, Vol. 27, No. 24. If you wish to obtain a copy of this article, please contact: *Gaming Today,* P.O. Box 93116, Las Vegas, NV 89193.

Acknowledgments

There are many people who have contributed in some way to this book, and have influenced my life. First, I wish to acknowledge my dear mother, because her life has been of such profound meaning, and of such complexity, that her story is a book in itself. It is an everlasting credit to her that she has not only retained her life and her sanity, but that she was so able to continually contribute to and foster our family. She is by far the most deserving person to whom I can offer my thanks.

I also wish to thank my literary agents, Greg Dinkin and Frank Scatoni. Greg is an accomplished author in his own right; Frank, a widely respected book editor. Through their agency, Venture Literary, they recognized the value of what I had to offer as an author of books on casino games and gaming. Without their efforts, this book, and the others in this series, would never have come to exist.

My thanks also to Bruce Bender, at Kensington Publishing Group, who has published this book and this series. He recognized that this book, and this series, offer valuable insight into the casino games as they really are, and that this book will enable almost all players to finally realize a happy and profitable casino experience. I thank Bruce, and the staff of Kensington, for their help in this process, and in particular to that wonderful lady, the lovely Ann LaFarge, my editor.

I also wish to thank my friend, fellow author, and gaming columnist John Grochowski, for his thoughts and help in providing a review of the manuscript. I have enjoyed reading John's works for a long time, and I find his words and thoughts of considerable value.

These sentiments also extend to my other fellow columnists from *Midwest Gaming & Travel* magazine: Henry Tamburin and Frank Scoblete, both well known authors of many books on casino gaming and casino games. Also thanks to my other colleagues and staff at the magazine, particularly Cathy Jaeger and Beth Wesselhoeft. Cathy and I have known each other for a long time, and she was at one time also the editor of several other magazines that published my articles. Since 1984 I have published a continuous column on casino gaming in various publications, and for most of these years it was Cathy who was my editor and friend. And darling Beth, well, she always calls me and reminds me of my deadline for my magazine column, and without her I would most likely have forgotten the month, and not just the day.

I am also fortunate to bring you a list of my friends, and others, who have helped me and influenced my life in many ways.

I extend my gratitude and thanks to my long-time friend Tom Caldwell for the many things he has done to help me, and enrich my life. I have had many discussions with Tom about casino games, and my thoughts about the games have become more mature because of these discussions. I also send my thanks to Norreta, Sean, and Brent, for reasons they all know.

To all my other friends and associates in the gaming business, from owners, managers, senior executives, hosts, and supervisors—you all know who you are, and I thank you.

My friends in Australia, Neil and his family, Lilli and little MRM (Mark), Ormond College, University of Melbourne, the Governor of Victoria and my former Master, Sir Davis McCaughey. Also his Proctorial Eminence R. A. Dwyer, Esq., and the Alumni Association of the University of Wollongong, NSW, Department of Philosophy, and Professor Chipman.

My grateful appreciation I also extend to Mr. Laurence E. Levit, C.P.A., of Los Angeles, who has been my steadfast friend, accountant, and adviser for two decades, and whose faith in me and my work has never faltered. A truer friend a man rarely finds. Also to Mr. Michael Harrison, attorney-at-law in Beverly Hills, California, whose expertise and help have made my life more secure.

To Andrew Hooker and the "Cowboys" from Vietnam, I also send my thanks. As well as to Edwin Slogar, a good friend.

I also wish to extend my sincere thanks and appreciation to Mrs. Ursula Steinberg for her valuable help and assistance.

Finally, to all those whose paths have crossed with mine, and who have for one reason or another stopped a while and visited. I may no longer remember your names, but I do remember what it meant to have those moments.

Thank you!

Index